Student Interactive

myView
LITERACY
2

SAVVAS
LEARNING COMPANY

ISBN-13: 978-0-134-90880-9
ISBN-10: 0-134-90880-5

4 20

Julie Coiro, Ph.D.

Jim Cummins, Ph.D.

Pat Cunningham, Ph.D.

Elfrieda Hiebert, Ph.D.

Pamela Mason, Ed.D.

Ernest Morrell, Ph.D.

P. David Pearson, Ph.D.

Frank Serafini, Ph.D.

Alfred Tatum, Ph.D.

Sharon Vaughn, Ph.D.

Judy Wallis, Ed.D.

Lee Wright, Ed.D.

UNIT 1

CONTENTS

You Are Here

CONTENTS

Nature's Wonders

You Are Here

Essential Question

How do different places affect us?

▶ **Watch**

"My Neighborhood" What places can you see in the video?

TURN and **TALK** What did you notice about these places? Describe the key ideas you learned.

SAVVAS realize™

Go ONLINE for all lessons.

▶ VIDEO

🔊 AUDIO

🎮 GAME

✏ ANNOTATE

📖 BOOK

🔍 RESEARCH

Reading Workshop

Reading-Writing Bridge

- Academic Vocabulary
- Read Like a Writer, Write for a Reader
- Spelling • Language and Conventions

Writing Workshop

Writing Workshop
- Introduce and Immerse
- Develop Elements • Develop Structure
- Writer's Craft • Publish, Celebrate, and Assess

Project-Based Inquiry

- Inquire • Research • Collaborate

Independent Reading

What can you do to become a good reader? Read, read, and read some more! On the next page, keep track of your independent reading.

Follow these steps to help you select a book you will enjoy reading on your own.

1. Ask: What is my purpose for reading?

• for fun?

• to learn something?

• to read something by my favorite author?

2. Select a book. Open it to any page and read it. Hold up a finger for each word you do not know. Then check this list:

1 Finger: Easy!

2 Fingers: Just right.

3 Fingers: Just right.

4 Fingers: A little too hard for now.

5 Fingers: Save for later.

My Reading Log

Date	Book	Pages Read	Minutes Read	My Ratings
				☺ ☺ ☹
				☺ ☺ ☹
				☺ ☺ ☹
				☺ ☺ ☹
				☺ ☺ ☹

Unit Goals

In this unit, you will

- read realistic fiction
- begin to write in your Writing Club
- learn about different places

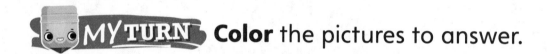 **Color** the pictures to answer.

	👍	👎
I know about realistic fiction and understand its elements.		
I can use language to make connections between reading and writing.		
I can plan, draft, and publish my writing.		
I can talk with others about how different places affect us.		

Academic Vocabulary

| affect | different | compare | location | region |

In this unit, you will read about **different** places. You will think about how these places **affect** people, or how they make people feel. You will also **compare** one **location** with another in a different **region**.

TURN and TALK Use the Academic Vocabulary words to talk with your partner. Compare the places you see in the pictures. Talk about how each place affects you. How does it make you feel?

Seeing Stars

You can see a lot more stars in the country than in the city.

Why is that?

Milky Way

Night sky far away from outside lights
There are about 3,000 stars above any spot on Earth in the night sky. Because there is no light pollution far from the city lights, in the country you can see all those stars!

Night sky in most cities

In most neighborhoods, people can see only 200 to 300 stars. In some cities, you can see only about 12 stars!

Most people in the United States cannot see our galaxy, the Milky Way. Why not?

Lights on buildings and streets cause light pollution. All that extra light keeps you from seeing the stars.

Weekly Question

What can we understand about a place when we look at it closely?

Quick Write What do you notice about the places in the pictures? Which picture shows a night sky like the one you see where you live? How would you feel if you visited a place where the night sky is different?

Listen for Long and Short Vowels

SEE and SAY Say the name of each picture. Listen to the vowel sound in the middle. Distinguish between the long and short vowel sounds.

Which picture name has a short vowel sound?

Which picture name has a long vowel sound?

TURN and TALK Work with a partner. Say the name of each picture. Underline the pictures with short vowel sounds.

Words with Short Vowels

When you see a word with a consonant-vowel-consonant pattern (CVC), the vowel usually has a short sound.

cap

MY TURN Read, or decode, the words below. Listen for the short vowel sounds.

Short a	Short e	Short i	Short o	Short u
cat	hen	zip	job	cub
bag	bed	win	top	run
man	leg	sit	dot	hum

TURN and TALK Read the words with a partner. Use them in sentences. Can you use all the words in one sentence?

hat	red	did	not	bug

Words with Short Vowels

MY TURN Look at each picture. Write the missing vowels to complete the words. Then read, or decode, each word.

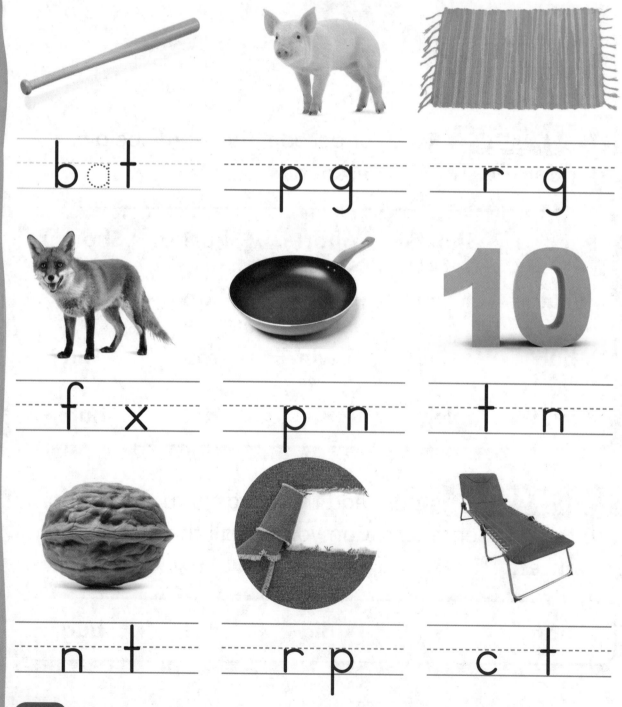

b a t   p g   r g

f x   p n   t n

n t   r p   c t

My Words to Know

MY TURN Some words are used often. These words are called high-frequency words. You will have to remember these words. Often, you can't sound them out. Read the high-frequency words in the box. Complete the sentences with the words.

which	each	than

1. _Which_ dog is your favorite?

2. I think that _____ dog is cute.

3. Do you know _____ one is older?

4. The tan one is older _____ the black one.

TURN and TALK Write the words on cards. Practice reading them with a partner.

I can read realistic fiction and understand setting.

Spotlight on Genre

Realistic Fiction

Realistic fiction tells a made-up story that could be real. It has characters, events that seem real, and a setting. The **setting** of a story tells when and where the story happens. Text and illustrations can help you understand the setting.

The setting is important. It can affect how characters act. In this story, the setting is a cottage by the sea. The character, Anna, is happy because this morning she will walk to the beach.

where

when

Anna and her sister were staying in a seaside cottage with Grandma for the whole summer. This morning, the three of them were walking to the beach to find shells for Anna's collection. Anna couldn't wait to get started.

TURN and TALK Talk about a story you have read. What was the setting of the story? Describe the importance of the setting.

REALISTIC FICTION ANCHOR CHART

Characters

Setting

◎ Where the story happens   ◎ When it happens

⸭ The setting can affect what the characters do. ⸭

Events

How Many Stars in the Sky?

Preview Vocabulary

Look for these words as you read *How Many Stars in the Sky?*

backyard	treehouse	searchlights	daylight

First Read

Look at the pictures.

Ask yourself questions about the story.

Read to understand the story.

Talk about the story with a partner.

Meet the illustrator

James E. Ransome is an artist who has won many awards for his drawings and books. As a child, he loved to draw cartoons! He also drew pictures of cars and many other things.

How Many Stars in the Sky?

By Lenny Hort
Paintings by James E. Ransome

 AUDIO

Audio with Highlighting

 ANNOTATE

1 **H**ow many stars in the sky?

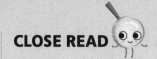

2   Mama was away that night and I couldn't sleep. Mama knows all about the sun and stars. But she was away and I didn't want to wake Daddy. So I stared out the window asking myself: How many stars in the sky?

3   I could count so many just from my room. I leaned out the window and I could count even more. That was just gazing over the backyard. How many stars in the sky?

Copyright © SAVVAS Learning Company LLC. All Rights Reserved.

Describe and Understand Setting

<u>Underline</u> the words that tell where the boy is.

backyard a yard behind a house

Use Text Evidence

Highlight words in the text that answer the question, "Why can't the boy count all the stars?"

4   I went outside with a pad and pencil. I started to count. I filled up one whole page of the pad.

5   But there were lots of stars hidden behind the trees. The house blocked out even more. The streetlamp was so bright I couldn't see stars anywhere near it. How many stars in the sky?

6   I climbed high up into my treehouse. I started at the Big Dipper and counted in a great circle all around the sky. I filled up page after page of the pad.

7   But when I got back to the Dipper it wasn't where I remembered it. I must have been out so long that the stars had moved. Old ones had set. New ones had risen. How many stars in the sky?

CLOSE READ

treehouse a small space built in the branches of a tree for children to play in or on

8   I climbed down from the treehouse and there was Daddy. "I couldn't sleep," I said.

9   "I can't sleep either," he said. "Your mama won't be back till tomorrow."

10   I told him how I wanted to count all the stars in the sky.

11   "If your mama was here," Daddy said, "I bet she'd know. Maybe you and I can find someplace where it'll be easier to count them."

12 My dog hopped in the truck with us and we drove into town. The streets were quiet, but lots of streetlights were burning. We could see the bright city skyline in the distance.

Describe and Understand Setting

<u>Underline</u> the sentence that describes what the town is like. Tell how the picture supports this description.

Use Text Evidence

Highlight the words that tell why the boy wants to go to a different place to see stars.

13 Daddy and I counted twenty-five or twenty-six stars. He said he thought one of them was the planet Jupiter. "This isn't a good place to see stars," I said.

14 "It's not a bad place to count them, though," he said. "But it's still too hard. Let's go where it'll be really easy."

15 We drove into the city. The big clock by
    the tunnel said 2:45, but neither one of
    us felt like sleeping.

Vocabulary in Context

You can figure out the meaning of a word you don't know from words in the same sentence or in sentences near it. <u>Underline</u> words that help you figure out the meaning of **dazzling.**

searchlights
powerful lights that can shine in any direction

16　We parked by Mama's office. There was a department store with brightly lit displays in every window. There were streetlamps on every corner.

17　There were dazzling neon signs. Headlights flashed from a steady stream of cars. Powerful searchlights beamed from the roofs of the skyscrapers.

18   And I couldn't see any stars at all.
"I count exactly one," said Daddy. "No,
wait," he said, "it's an airplane."

19   "Maybe the stars just don't want to be
counted," I said.

20   We drove back through the tunnel.
I was tired, and I thought we were going
home. But instead, Daddy drove us
deep into the country.

21   There weren't any cars. There weren't any streetlights. There weren't any houses. Even the moon had set. And I knew we could never count all the stars.

Describe and Understand Setting

Underline the sentences that tell what the country is like.

CLOSE READ

Use Text Evidence

Highlight the words that show the boy sees lots of stars.

22   No matter where I looked, new ones appeared every time I blinked my eyes. Daddy pointed up above and showed me the Milky Way. The stars were so thick I couldn't tell one from another.

23 We were much too tired to drive anymore, so we slept underneath the stars that night.

Describe and Understand Setting

<u>Underline</u> the words that tell you when the boy and his father wake up. Examine the picture to see how it supports this description.

daylight the natural light of day

24 It was daylight when we woke. "Daddy," I said, "all those stars are always out there even when we can't see them, right?"

25 "Of course they are," he said.

26 "Can we try to count them again some time?" I asked.

27 "Any night you feel like it," he said, "you and me and Mama can all go out together."

28 I could hardly wait to see Mama and tell her about it. In a little while we'd all be back home. But now I was glad just to be standing there with Daddy, basking in the warmth of the one star we could see—

29 and that was the Sun.

Develop Vocabulary

A **compound word** is made up of two shorter words. Use the meanings of the shorter words to predict the meaning of the compound word.

MY TURN Use the shorter words to define each compound word. Write your definition. Then find each word in the story. Read the definition. Is your definition correct? Change it if you need to.

Compound Word	My Definition
backyard	a yard in the back of a house
treehouse	
searchlights	
daylight	

TURN and TALK Use the shorter words to predict the meanings of these compound words: **birdhouse, lighthouse, housefly.** Check the meanings in a dictionary.

Check for Understanding

MY TURN Look back at the text to answer the questions. Write the answers.

1. What makes this text realistic fiction?

_____

- -

_____

- -

_____

2. Why do you think the author has the boy and his dad try to look at the stars from different places?

_____

- -

_____

- -

_____

3. Why can they see so many more stars in the country?

_____

- -

_____

- -

_____

Describe and Understand Setting

The **setting** is where and when a story happens.

MY TURN Go to the Close Read notes in the text. Underline details about the settings. Use details you underlined to describe the importance of each setting.

Setting	Description of Setting	Why This Setting Is Important
the boy's room	It's night; the room has a bed and a window.	
the town		
the country at night		
the country in daylight		

Use Text Evidence

Using **text evidence** can help you describe the importance of the settings in a story.

MY TURN Go back to the Close Read notes on text evidence. Follow the directions to highlight the text. Use the text evidence you highlight to support your responses in the chart below.

Setting	Is this a good place to see stars?	Why?
outside the boy's house		
the town		
the country		

Reflect and Share

Talk About It

You read about places a boy and his father went to look at stars. Where would you like to go to see stars? Why? Use examples from the texts to support your response.

Make Comments and Build on Ideas

When having a discussion, it is important to share your ideas and listen to the ideas of others.

- Take turns talking.

- Build on the ideas of others.

Use these sentence starters to help you build on the ideas of others.

I'm glad you said that because . . .
I agree with you, and I also think . . .

Weekly Question

What can we understand about a place when we look at it closely?

I can use language to make connections between reading and writing.

My Learning Goal

Academic Vocabulary

Related words are words that share word parts. Related words have related meanings.

MY TURN Use a dictionary to find the meanings of each pair of related words. Then choose which word should complete the sentence.

Related Words: different/difference

There is a big difference

between an apple and an orange.

Related Words: locate/location

A good _____

for a library is near a school.

Related Words: compare/comparison

My parents _____

prices when they shop.

Read Like a Writer, Write for a Reader

Authors create a voice when they write. The words a character says show how the character sounds and what kind of person the character is.

Boy's Words from Story	Without the Boy's Voice
"Mama was away that night and I couldn't sleep."	My mother was not at home, and I was not able to sleep.

MY TURN Rewrite this sentence so that it sounds like a young character.

I am sure my mother will be waiting for us to arrive at our house.

_____

- - - - - - - - - - - - - - - - - -

_____

_____

- - - - - - - - - - - - - - - - - -

_____

_____

- - - - - - - - - - - - - - - - - -

_____

Spell Words with Short Vowels

Short vowel sounds are usually spelled with a single vowel: **a, e, i, o,** or **u.**

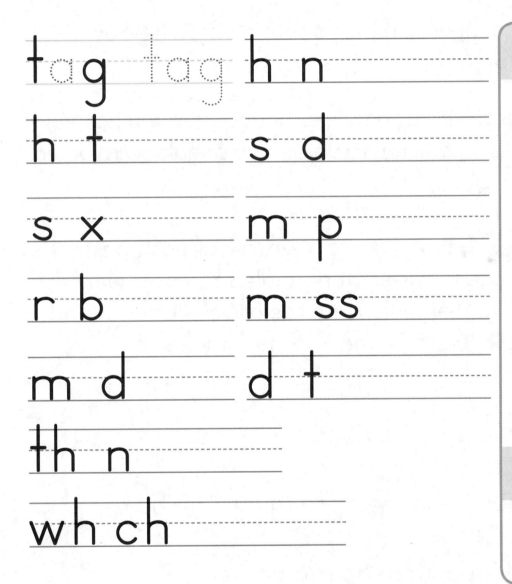 **MY TURN** Write the missing vowel to make a word from the word lists. Then write the word.

t a g   t a g   h _ n

h _ t   s _ d

s _ x   m _ p

r _ b   m _ ss

m _ d   d _ t

th _ n

wh _ ch

Spelling Words

six

tag

rib

map

mess

dot

mud

hen

sad

hot

My Words to Know

which

than

Simple Sentences

A **simple sentence** tells one complete thought. It starts with a capital letter. It ends with the correct end mark. The subject and verb must agree with one another in number.

Read this simple sentence about a boy: **The boy counts stars.**

The sentence tells a complete thought about a boy who counts stars. The singular subject and singular verb agree.

MY TURN Edit this draft. Cross out each part you need to change to correct the simple sentences with subject-verb agreement. Write the correct letter or end mark above it. The first one is done for you.

A
~~a~~ boy went for a walk. he found.

A dime The dime were shiny The boy.

picked it up then he ran home.

I can plan, draft, and publish my writing.

My Learning Goal

Meet the Author

Authors are regular people, just like you. They may like the same things you like. They may do the same things you do. You can read about authors. Often the back of a book tells you about the author. Sometimes a page inside the book gives you author information.

Get to know the authors of some books in your classroom library. As you read about each author, think about these things:

- interesting facts about the author
- the author's family or pets
- things the author likes
- how the author gets ideas for books
- how the author writes a book

TURN and TALK Share something you learned about an author with a partner.

What Good Writers Do

Good writers follow steps in a plan.

Here are some steps you can follow in Writing Workshop. You can:

1. Get ideas from things that happen in your life.

   - reading information in a book
   - brainstorming with other people

2. Write your ideas in your writer's notebook.

3. Have a conference to share your ideas:

   - with your teacher
   - with your peers in Writing Club

4. Use what you learned in a conference to revise your writing.

Writing Club

Writing Club is where you can talk with your peers about your writing. You talk about their writing too. As a member of Writing Club, you have an important job.

MY TURN You are going to have Writing Club today.

Here are some skills you can practice.

- ☐ Listen carefully to what others say.

- ☐ Ask questions if you do not understand something.

- ☐ Tell what you like about your classmates' writing.

- ☐ Tell what your classmates can do to make their writing better.

- ☐ Give feedback that is clear and useful.

- ☐ Be polite when you give feedback.

We Make Our Neighborhood Better

We started a community garden. We all work in it and share the food we grow!

We are all working together to design a new playground! It's going to be great!

Weekly Question

How can people improve their neighborhoods?

TURN and TALK

How are these people making their neighborhood a better place? What ideas could you try in your own neighborhood?

> We know our neighbors' names and phone numbers.

> We turn on our porch lights when the sun goes down.

Listen for Long and Short Vowels

SEE and SAY Say the name of each picture. Listen to the vowel sound in the middle. Distinguish between the long and short vowel sounds.

What is the vowel sound in the first picture?
Is it short or long?

What is the vowel sound in the second picture?
Is it short or long?

TURN and TALK Work with a partner. Say the name of each picture. Underline the pictures with long vowel sounds.

Long Vowels: CVCe

When you see a consonant-vowel-consonant-**e** pattern (CVCe), the vowel usually has a long sound, and the **e** is silent. Read, or decode, these words aloud.

game

Long a	Long e	Long i	Long o	Long u
bake	Pete	pipe	rode	cute
tape	these	wide	hose	mule
awake	delete	arise	alone	amuse

TURNand**TALK** Read these sentences with a partner. Find the CVCe words with long vowels.

I like a safe place to ride my bike.

I awoke and ate a huge pile of pancakes in my robe.

Long Vowels: CVCe

MY TURN Read, or decode, the words in the box. Then use one of the words to answer each clue.

nine	joke	nose	cube	escape

1. It is on your face. ___nose___

2. It comes before ten. _____

3. It has six sides. _____

4. It makes you laugh. _____

5. It is a way out. _____

MY TURN On a sheet of paper, write a sentence that contains two of the words from the box. Give it to a partner to read.

My Words to Know

MY TURN Read the words in the box. Then write a sentence using each word. One is done for you.

called	long	most

1. Pencils are long and thin.

2. _____

3. _____

4. _____

TURN and TALK Read your sentences aloud to a partner. Find the new word in each sentence. Help each other correct any mistakes.

My Learning Goal

I can read realistic fiction and understand its characters.

Spotlight on Genre

Realistic Fiction

Realistic fiction has **characters** who look and act like real people. Both the text and illustrations can help you understand the characters.

TURN and TALK Tell a partner about a realistic fiction story you have read. Who are the characters? In what ways do they act like real people?

Be a Fluent Reader Fluent readers read at a good rate. Practice reading aloud.

Here are some tips for fluent reading:

- Don't read too slowly.
- Don't read too quickly either. Read as if you are speaking.
- Use commas and periods to help you read. Pause at commas. Stop at periods.

Realistic Fiction Anchor Chart

Authors tell us about characters.

How they look

What they do

Characters

What they say

What they think

How they feel

Maybe Something Beautiful

Preview Vocabulary

Look for these words as you read *Maybe Something Beautiful.*

joy	shadows	scurried	rhythm	splattered

First Read

Read to understand the text.

Look at illustrations to help you understand what you read.

Ask what this text is about.

Talk about the text with a partner.

Meet the Author

F. Isabel Campoy writes poetry, stories, plays, and biographies. She writes in both English and Spanish, and many of her books are about Hispanic culture. She has coauthored many award-winning books, including *Yes! We Are Latinos* and *¡Pío Peep!*

Maybe Something
BEAUTIFUL

HOW ART TRANSFORMED A NEIGHBORHOOD

BY **F. Isabel Campoy**
AND **Theresa Howell**

iLLUSTRATED BY
Rafael López

🔊 AUDIO
Audio with Highlighting
✐ ANNOTATE

CLOSE READ

1 In the heart of a gray city, there lived a girl who loved to doodle, draw, color, and paint.

2 Every time she saw a blank piece of paper, Mira thought to herself, *Hmm, maybe . . .*

3 And because of this, her room was filled with color and her heart was filled with joy.

joy a feeling of great happiness

62

4   On her way to school one day,
     Mira gave a round apple to Mr. Henry,
     the owner of the shop down the street.

5   She gave a flower to Ms. López,
     the lady with the sparkling eyes.

Ask and Answer Questions

Highlight any text details about Mira that you have questions about.

6   She gave a songbird to Mr. Sax and a red heart to the policeman who walked up and down the streets.

7   On her way home, Mira taped a glowing sun onto the wall hiding in the shadows.

8   Her city was less gray—but not much.

shadows shaded places away from light

CLOSE READ

9 The next day, Mira saw a man with a pocket full of paintbrushes.

10 He gazed at the wall.

11 He looked at her sun.

12 He held his fingers up in a square and peered through them.

13 "Hmm . . .," he said thoughtfully.

14 "What do you see?" Mira asked.

15 "Maybe . . . something beautiful," the man replied.

Vocabulary in Context

Sometimes the author gives you a synonym for an unfamiliar word. A synonym is a word that means the same or nearly the same as another word. <u>Underline</u> the word that means nearly the same as **gazed**.

16 Then, just like that, he dipped a brush in the paint.

BAM! POW!

17 The shadows scurried away.

18 Sky blue cut through the gloom.

19 The man's laughter was like a rainbow spreading across the sky.

Describe and Understand Characters
Underline the word that shows the man is happy to be painting.

scurried moved quickly

20 "Who are you?" Mira asked.

21 "I'm an artist," he said. "A muralist.

22 I paint on walls!"

23 "I'm an artist too," she told him.

24 He handed Mira a brush.

25 "THEN COME ON!"

Mira dipped it in the loudest color she saw.

YOW-WEE!

The wall lit up like sunshine.

CLOSE READ

Describe and Understand Characters

Underline the word that helps you know how Mira feels.

Vocabulary in Context

<u>Underline</u> the word in the first sentence that has nearly the same meaning as **pizzazz**.

rhythm the strong beat that some music has

29 As the man drew pictures on the bricks, Mira added color, punch, and pizzazz!

30 Soon Mr. Sax joined in.

31 Then came others.

32 Everyone painted to the rhythm.

33 Salsa, merengue, bebop!

34 Even Mira's mama painted
and danced the cha-cha-cha!

35 The whole neighborhood
became a giant block party.

36 Until . . .

Describe and Understand Characters

Underline the words that tell what Mira thinks when she first sees the policeman.

37 . . . the policeman walked up.

38 "Excuse me," he said.

39 The music stopped. Mira put her brush down.

40 They were surely in trouble.

41 The officer cleared his throat, then paused.

42 "May I paint with you?" he asked.

43 So Mira handed him a paintbrush.

44 And the music started again.

45 Teachers and papas jumped in.

46 Babies too!

47 Mira and the man handed out brush after brush.

48 Color spread throughout the streets.

49 So did joy.

50 Wherever Mira and the man went, art followed like the string of a kite.

51 After they colored the walls, they painted utility boxes and benches.

52 They decorated sidewalks with poetry and shine.

53 And everyone danced.

54 Together, they created something more beautiful than they had ever imagined.

Ask and Answer Questions

Highlight a text detail that you can ask a question about.

CLOSE READ

splattered
splashed by dots of
something

55   When their clothes were splattered
with a million colors, everyone sat down
to rest—except the muralist.

56   His eyes sparkled.

57   "You, my friends, are all artists," he
told them.

58   "The world is your canvas."

59   He smiled wide, then pulled
everything together in big, sweeping
motions.

60   His paintbrush was like a magic wand.

61 When he was finished, Mira added one more bird, way up in the sky.

62 Maybe, she thought. Just maybe . . .

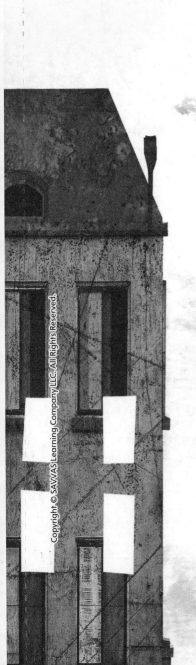

Ask and Answer Questions

What questions do you have about how the story ends? Highlight a text detail that you can ask a question about.

Fluency

Read aloud paragraphs 1 to 8 of the story several times with a partner. Practice reading at the same rate you talk, not too fast and not too slow.

77

Develop Vocabulary

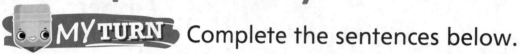 Complete the sentences below.

1. People can see their **shadows** when the sun

   is out .

2. _____ brings me **joy**.

3. The _____ **scurried** away with
   tiny bits of food.

Use the words **splattered** and **rhythm** to describe the
man who painted murals.

Check for Understanding

MY TURN Look back at the text to answer the questions. Write the answers.

1. What about this story could happen in real life?

_____

_____

_____

2. How do the illustrations help you understand the story?

_____

_____

_____

3. How is the neighborhood different at the end of the story than it was at the beginning?

_____

_____

_____

Describe and Understand Characters

Characters are the people or animals in stories.
Traits are features of characters.

- External traits are what characters look like, how they act, and what they say.

- Internal traits are what characters think and feel.

MY TURN Go to the Close Read notes about characters. Follow the directions to underline the text. Use what you underlined to complete the chart. Then describe the characters' internal and external traits.

Details I Underlined	Character	Trait It Shows
laughter	the man	He laughs loudly. He is happy to be painting.

Ask and Answer Questions

Active readers ask and answer questions to understand the characters and events in a story.

MY TURN Go back to the Close Read notes. Follow the directions. Write questions you have as you read and highlight the text. Then use text evidence to answer your questions after you read.

Questions I Had During Reading	Answers

Reflect and Share

Write to Sources

You read how Mira and other people improved the places where they lived. On a separate piece of paper, compose a letter to your neighbors explaining how you would like to improve your neighborhood. Use examples from texts you have read this week to support your ideas.

Write Correspondence

A friendly letter has five parts. Include them all.

- heading (September 8, 2019)

- greeting (Dear friend,)

- body (the letter's message)

- closing (Your friend,)

- signature (sign your name)

Think of how to make your neighborhood better. Write your ideas in a friendly letter to your neighbors. Use examples from the texts to explain your ideas.

Weekly Question

How can people improve their neighborhoods?

I can use language to make connections between reading and writing.

Academic Vocabulary

Synonyms are words that have the same or almost the same meaning.

MY TURN Write a word that is a synonym for each word.

Word	Synonym
affect	change
different	
location	

MY TURN Use a word and one of its synonyms in a new sentence. Then explain the meaning of the two words you used.

_____

- -

_____

- -

_____

Read Like a Writer, Write for a Reader

Authors usually tell stories in the order in which events happen. They use words and phrases that show time order. Authors use words such as **first**, **next**, and **last**. They also use words like **in the morning** or **after dinner** to help readers know when events happened. Here is an example from the text.

> "**When he was finished,** Mira added one more bird, way up in the sky."

MY TURN Tell what happened when you arrived at school this morning. Use words that show the order of events.

_____

_____

_____

_____

_____

_____

Spell Words with Long Vowels (CVCe)

Long vowels are often spelled with the pattern consonant-vowel-consonant-silent **e**.

 **MY TURN** Write the Spelling Words that rhyme.

cake   lake

rose

name

lime   dome

trade   chase

Then write the My Words to Know.

Spelling Words

time
lake
home
game
nose
rake
made
erase
hose
became

My Words to Know

called
long

Subjects and Predicates

A sentence has a subject and a predicate. The subject and the verb in the predicate agree in number.

The **subject** tells who or what does something.

Carmen rides the bus to school.

The **predicate** tells what the subject is or does.

Carmen rides the bus to school.

MY TURN Edit this draft. Make sure every sentence is a complete sentence with a subject and a verb that agree in number. Underline the sentence that is correct. Then write a subject or predicate for each sentence that needs one.

carries
Noah a large backpack. Is very heavy.

Five books in the backpack. His lunch is in the

backpack also. Noah's friends heavy

backpacks too.

I can plan, draft, and publish my writing.

A Writer's Notebook

A writer's notebook is a place to keep ideas you can use later in your writing. For example:

- interesting observations
- catchy words or phrases
- useful quotes
- drawings or pictures
- lists

You can also write drafts in a writer's notebook.

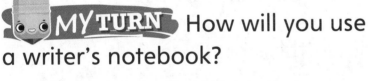 **MY TURN** How will you use a writer's notebook?

I am most excited about using a writer's notebook because

_____

- -

_____

_____

- -

_____

_____

- -

_____

Tools Authors Use

Authors use special tools to help them write well. Two tools are a dictionary and a thesaurus.

You can use a **dictionary** to find how to spell a word. Think of how the beginning of the word is likely spelled. Look up those letters first. You may need to try different spelling patterns for the sounds in the word.

You can use a **thesaurus** to find just the right word for what you want to say. The words in a thesaurus are in ABC order.

MY TURN Use a thesaurus to replace the underlined words. Write two possible words.

1. There is a <u>big</u> park down the street.

large _____

2. On Sundays, the park is <u>crowded</u> with people.

_____ _____

3. I am always <u>happy</u> to play there.

_____ _____

Digital Tools Authors Use

Digital, or computer, tools make writing more interesting. Examples are different fonts, colors, and images.

MY TURN Read both stories. Think about the ways the writer used digital tools in the second.

A Community Garden
    People on my street planted a community garden. We planted sunflowers that grew very tall. We planted corn, lettuce, and tomatoes. Everything tasted yummy!

A Community Garden

People on my street planted a community garden. We planted sunflowers that grew very TALL. We planted corn, lettuce, and tomatoes. Everything tasted yummy!

TURN and TALK How does using digital tools make the writing interesting? What can you do with digital tools to improve your writing?

Fighting Fires

Firefighters work to put out fires and rescue people. Each item firefighters wear helps keep them safe while they work. For example, their clothes are made from a special fabric that protects them from the high heat and flames. Firefighters' gear is very heavy!

helmet

air tank

mask

coat

gloves

pants

boots

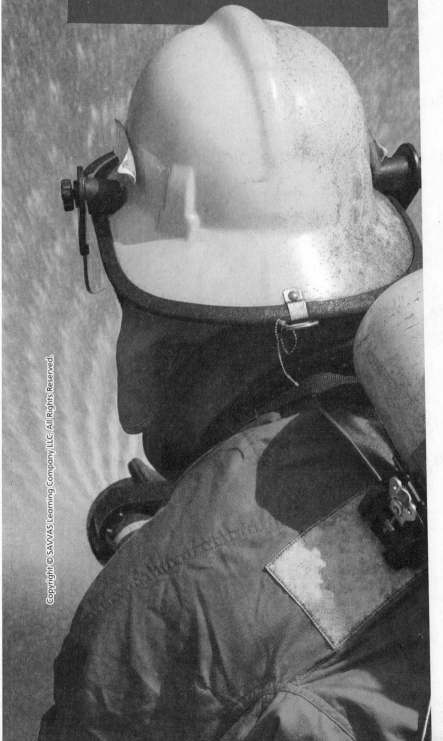

Firefighters must stay in shape and be ready to help. They practice and train a lot to carry their gear and help people.

Weekly Question

How does living in a community help people?

 **MY TURN**

Look at the diagram and picture. Read the information about firefighters. How do they help people? Why do firefighters need special training and gear?

Make Rhyming Words

 **SEE and SAY** Words rhyme when they have the same ending sound. Say the name of each picture.

What is the ending sound in each word?

Underline the picture that rhymes with the pictures above.

  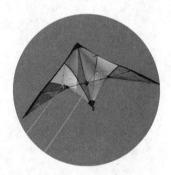

TURN and TALK Work with a partner. Say the word for each picture. Produce three or more words that rhyme with them.

Consonant Blends

Some words have two or three consonants whose sounds are blended together. For example, the **tr** in **train** and the **mp** in **lump** are blended in this way. These letter groups are called **consonant blends.**

Read each word below. Listen to the sounds of the consonants.

<u>s</u>poke	trip	clap	prize	flake
fast	lift	jump	grand	slant
scalp	scrub	split	strike	sprint

TURN and **TALK** Reread the words in the chart with a partner. <u>Underline</u> the consonant blend in each word. Some words have more than one consonant blend.

Consonant Blends

 **MY TURN** Unscramble the letters to write a word that names each picture. Then read the words.

mudr

lnatp

meils

drum

_____

_____

mutsp

tireps

gorf

_____

_____

_____

My Words to Know

MY TURN Read the words in the box. Find and underline them in the sentences below. Read each sentence. The first one is done for you.

more	things	sound

1. Drums sound loud.

2. Ted was still thirsty. He wanted more juice.

3. The shiny things in the box are seashells.

4. Did you hear that odd sound?

TURN and TALK Work with a partner. Take turns saying another sentence for each word.

Remember these words. You will read them a lot!

My Learning Goal

I can read about different places in my community.

Informational Text

An informational text tells **facts** and **details** about a **main**, or **central**, **idea**.

- The **main idea** is the most important idea in a text.

- Evidence in the text supports the main idea with more facts and examples.

Establish Purpose People read for a reason. One purpose, or reason, for reading an informational text is to learn new information on a topic. Before you begin to read, ask yourself what you want to learn.

TURN and **TALK** Talk about a purpose for reading *Places We Go*. What kind of information might you look for in this text? For example, you may want to learn which places the author will talk about. Set your own purpose for reading.

Informational Text Anchor Chart

 ## Main Idea

the most important idea
in a text or text part

Details

facts that support the
main idea

information that develops
the main idea

examples that illustrate
the main idea

Places We Go

Preview Vocabulary

Look for these words as you read the text from *Places We Go.*

community	services	librarian	supermarkets	hospital

First Read

Read for the purpose you set.

Look for the main idea of the text.

Ask questions to clarify information.

Talk about the most important ideas.

Meet the Author

Rachelle Kreisman won an award for her children's books about places, heroes, and activities in communities. In her Connecticut community, she enjoys hiking, kayaking, and other outdoor activities.

from
Places We Go

A KIDS' GUIDE TO COMMUNITY BUILDINGS

By Rachelle Kreisman

AUDIO

Audio with Highlighting

ANNOTATE

What Is a Community?

1   Hooray for the **community!** A community is a place where people live, work, and play. It is made up of neighborhoods. There, you will find homes and people. Who lives in one of those neighborhoods? You! That makes you part of a community.

2   People in a community help each other and work together. They share roads, parks, and buildings.

DiD YOU KNOW?

Three kinds of communities are urban, suburban, and rural. Urban areas are cities. They have tall buildings and many people. Suburban areas are near cities. People often live in houses and apartments. Rural areas have fewer people and more land. Farms and villages are often found there.

CLOSE READ

3   Can you name some buildings in a community? They include markets, schools, libraries, and hospitals. Many people work at those places. They provide goods and services. Goods are things that people can buy or borrow, such as food and books. Services are things that people do for each other. Teaching and medical care are services.

services work that people do to help others

School

4 Where do many kids go to learn? School! Most kids start Kindergarten around age five. That is the first year of elementary school.

5 Teachers plan lessons for many subjects. They teach math, reading, science, and social studies. Kids usually stay in one classroom for most of the day. They may go to other teachers for art, music, library, and gym.

6   Middle school often starts in grade six or seven. Then kids go to high school in ninth grade. High school lasts for four years. When students graduate, they get an award called a **diploma**.

7   Middle and high school kids have many teachers. Each teaches a different subject. Students may start the day in a homeroom class. *Ding!* A bell often tells them when it is time to change classes.

8   Schools are an important part of the community. They bring people together. Many students go to after-school activities. They join clubs and play sports. Some kids take part in plays, band, or chorus. People in the community can watch the sports games. They can also attend the plays and concerts.

Vocabulary in Context

Sometimes you can figure out the meaning of unfamiliar words by reading words nearby that you already know. Underline words in the text that help you understand what after-school activities are.

Use Text Evidence

Highlight words that tell why the library is a popular place in communities.

Library

9 The library is a popular place in communities. It is filled with thousands of books. A library's media center has movies, music, and sound recordings of books. People in the community can borrow the books and media for free. How can you do that? It's easy! Get a library card. It shows that you are a library member.

SANTA MARIA PUBLIC LIBRARY

10 Some people go to the library to read. Others go to do research. People also use computers there to go on the **Internet**. They may read news from home or email friends and family.

librarian a person in charge of a library

11   What if you need help at the library? No problem! You can ask a librarian to help you find books and other materials.

12   The librarian also plans programs for the community. Some members take part in book clubs. They read the same books and get together to talk about them. Authors may come by to talk and sign the books they wrote. Libraries may also show movies and host parties.

13 Have you ever been to the children's section of a library? It is where you will find books written just for kids.

14 The children's section often has story time. The librarian or other guests will read picture books aloud to visitors. Many libraries also have summer reading programs. Kids can sign up, read books, and win prizes.

CLOSE READ

Identify Main Idea

Underline the words that help you know the main idea of paragraphs 13 to 14.

Identify Main Idea

Underline the words that help you identify the main idea of this section.

supermarkets large stores that sell food and other goods

Grocery Store

15   Where do most people get the food they need? They go to the local grocery store. Large grocery stores are called supermarkets.

16 People find what they need by searching the aisles in a market. Signs often show what is found in each aisle.

17 Many people work in the grocery store. Trucks bring food and other items to the store. Workers unload boxes and stock the shelves. Cashiers work at the register. They scan items to tell people how much money they owe. Some workers put groceries in bags for shoppers.

Hospital

hospital a place where doctors and nurses care for sick or injured people

18 When people get sick or hurt, they may have to go to a hospital. It is open all day and night. Most hospitals are busy places with many workers. Doctors and nurses give patients medical care to help them get well.

19 If you go to a hospital, your parents will sign you in. You will get an ID bracelet with your name on it. First, you will see a nurse. Then a doctor will give you a checkup.

20 Do you need medical care right away? You can go to the hospital's emergency room. An ambulance may be called to take you there quickly. When the lights and siren are on, cars must move out of the way. Emergency medical workers take care of you on the way to the hospital.

Vocabulary in Context

Underline words that help you understand what an ambulance does.

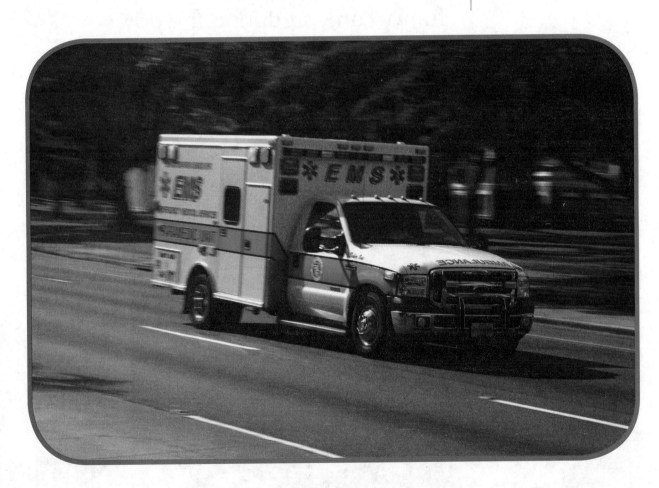

CLOSE READ

CLOSE READ

Use Text Evidence

Highlight words in the text that tell how a hospital is ready for patients who need to stay overnight.

21 A patient may need to stay overnight at the hospital. If that happens, the hospital is ready. Many rooms have beds for patients. They can watch TV and eat their meals in bed.

22 If you have to stay overnight, you will not be alone. At most hospitals, a parent can stay with you. Friends and family can visit during the day.

So Many Places

23 People have so many places to go for goods and services. That makes life in the community much easier. Lucky you! You get to attend school and go to the library. When you are older, you can get a job. With the money you earn, you can open a bank account. You can also use the money to buy things you need, such as food and gas.

Develop Vocabulary

MY TURN Use a print or digital dictionary to find the meanings and pronunciations of these words from *Places We Go*. With a partner, take turns saying aloud each word. Then write the meanings in your own words.

Word	Meaning
community	a place where people live and spend time
services	
librarian	ⓘ
supermarkets	where you get food
hospital	th elpr

Check for Understanding

MY TURN Look back at the text to answer the questions. Write the answers.

1. What makes this an informational text?

_____

_____

_____

_____

2. Why does the author include the headings School, Library, Grocery Store, and Hospital?

_____

_____

_____

_____

3. If you were starting a new community, which of these would you build first: a hospital, a library, a school, or a grocery store? Why?

_____

_____

_____

_____

Identify Main Idea

The topic of a text is what the text is about. The **main idea**, or central idea, is the most important idea about the topic. A paragraph or a section of text can also have a main idea.

MY TURN Go to the Close Read notes. Underline words that help you identify main ideas in the text. Your teacher can help you use what you underlined to complete the chart.

Paragraphs	Topic	Main Idea
1–3	Community	A community is where people live, work, play, and help each other.
9–14		
15–17		

Use Text Evidence

Authors include evidence to support their main ideas. Use text evidence to understand the main ideas in an informational text.

MY TURN Go back to the Close Read notes. Highlight the supporting evidence that helps you understand main ideas. Use what you highlighted to complete the chart.

Supporting Evidence	Main Idea
They teach math, reading, science, and social studies.	Teachers in elementary schools plan lessons for many subjects.

Reflect and Share

Talk About It

How are the places in your community the same as the ones you read about this week? How are they different? Use examples from the texts to support your response.

Listen to Others

In a discussion, it is important to listen to everyone. Before you talk, listen to what others have to say.

- Don't interrupt.

- Listen carefully to the ideas of others.

Use these sentence starters to help you build on the ideas of others.

You're right about . . .
I agree with . . . ,
but I also think . . .

Weekly Question

How does living in a community help people?

I can use language to make connections between reading and writing.

My Learning Goal

Academic Vocabulary

Context clues are words and sentences near an unfamiliar word that can help you understand it.

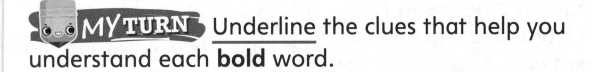 **MY TURN** Underline the clues that help you understand each **bold** word.

1. Being in a beautiful place can **affect** a person. It can change a person's bad mood into a good one.

2. It's good to visit **different** places and not always go to the same place.

3. When you visit a new place, you can **compare** it to your home to see how it is the same.

4. A trip to a new **location**, or place, can teach you something.

5. Every **region** is special. If you can, visit another part of the world and see what it's like.

Read Like a Writer, Write for a Reader

An author has a main idea. The main idea is the most important idea in a text. The author includes details that help explain or support that main idea.

Text from *Places We Go*	Main Idea and Details
"Many people work in the grocery store. Trucks bring food and other items to the store. Workers unload boxes and stock the shelves. Cashiers work at the register. … Some workers put groceries in bags for shoppers."	The first sentence tells me the author's main idea. Each sentence that follows is a detail about people who work in the grocery store.

MY TURN Write two details that explain this main idea: People go to the library for different reasons.

_____

- -

_____

- -

_____

Spell Words with Consonant Blends

Some words have two or three consonants whose sounds are blended together. For example, **s** and **l** are blended together in **slip.**

MY TURN Write a Spelling Word with the same beginning or ending consonant blend as each word.

brave   brick

frame _____

blip _____

fist _____

stray _____

rust _____

stop _____

spin _____

spray _____

scrub _____

Write the word that rhymes with each word.

pound _____

wings _____

Spelling Words

nest

past

spend

spring

strong

scrap

frog

blog

stick

brick

My Words to Know

sound

things

Compound Sentences

Sometimes the ideas in two sentences are related. The sentences can be combined to make one **compound sentence**, using a comma and the word **and**, **but**, or **or**.

Two sentences	Compound sentence
I have a library card. I use it every week.	I have a library card, **and** I use it every week.
We can bring a lunch to school. We can eat the school lunch.	We can bring a lunch to school, **or** we can eat the school lunch.

MY TURN Cross out the end mark between simple sentences that can be combined into a compound sentence. Add a **comma** and the connecting word **and, but**, or **or**. Change capital letters if you need to.

, and it

Our town has a park. It is near my house. I like to go there after school. I must do my homework first. Then I meet my friends at the park. We have fun together. We play on the playground. We play ball.

I can plan, draft, and publish my writing.

The Structure of a Fiction Text

Authors can choose to write different kinds of texts. Fiction is one kind. Fiction is a made-up story. These are some traits of a fiction story:

- **Characters** are the people or animals in the story.

- **Setting** is the time and place of the story.

- **Plot** is what happens in the beginning, middle, and end.

- In most stories the characters have a **problem**, and they must find a **resolution** to the problem.

MY TURN Choose a fiction book from your classroom library. Complete the sentences about it.

_____

_____

is a fiction book. I know it is fiction because

_____

_____

_____

The Structure of a Nonfiction Text

Nonfiction is another kind of text. Nonfiction tells about real events. In a nonfiction book you may find:

- names of real people and places

- main ideas and details

- text features such as headings and captions

- graphic features such as photographs, maps, and diagrams

You will find nonfiction books together in the library.

MY TURN Choose a nonfiction book from your classroom library. Complete the sentences about it.

_____

- -

_____

is a nonfiction book. I know it is nonfiction because

_____

- -

_____

- -

_____

- -

Digital Tools Authors Use

You can write your stories and other texts on paper. There are also many ways to use a computer to publish your writing digitally. Here are some examples:

Digital Tool	Good to Use
computer printout	to give copies to classmates, friends, and family
e-book	to create a book, even including sound and video, to share with others digitally
classroom Web site	to share your writing with school friends and families digitally
blog	to share your writing with many people digitally

COLLABORATE With a partner, use a digital tool to publish your writing.

City Sights

Folks say my city is crowded and loud.
I say the bustling noise makes me proud.

Honks and whistles, shouts and beeps,
I love my city. It never sleeps!

Thick, rich smells, so spicy and sweet,
Oh, how I smile as I walk down the street.

Seeing glass buildings that reach to the sky.
Hearing the shouts of kids passing by.

These are some of the things I adore.
Do you like the city? Is there a place you
like more?

Weekly Question

How do different places make us feel?

Quick Write People live in small towns and big cities. Think about the place where you live. What feelings do you have when you think about it? How are your feelings similar to those expressed in the poem "City Sights"?

Make Rhyming Words

 **SEE** *and* **SAY** Words rhyme when they end in the same sounds. Say the name of each picture.

What are the ending sounds in each word?
Do the words rhyme?
Name other words that rhyme with the pictures above.

 **TURN** *and* **TALK** Work with a partner. Say the name of each picture. See how many rhyming words you can make for each picture.

Consonant Digraphs ch, sh, wh, th, ph and Trigraph tch

Sometimes two or three consonants make one sound.

chick   **sh**ip   **wh**ip

thorn   **ph**one   wa**tch**

MY TURN Read, or decode, the words below.

| check lunch | shake fish | when white | thin, tooth there, smooth | photo graph | match pitch |

TURN and TALK Reread the words aloud with a partner. Then choose two words and use both words in a sentence. Share your sentences.

Consonant Digraphs ch, sh, wh, th, ph and Trigraph tch

MY TURN Use a consonant group from the box to complete the word in each sentence. Read the words.

ch	sh	wh	th	ph	tch

1. That is a very good  oto of you.

2. This story is about a _____ ale in the sea.

3. Put the books back on the _____ elf.

4. Zane ran fast to ca _____ the ball.

5. Let's walk on the pa _____ down to the lake.

6. The cat sat by the big green _____ air.

My Words to Know

MY TURN Read the words in the box. Find and <u>underline</u> the words in the story. The first one is done for you. Then read the story.

great	before	means

Emily did a <u>great</u> job on the spelling test. She studied a lot before the test. Her teacher is proud of her. That means a lot to Emily. She feels great.

TURN and TALK With a partner, write another story with the words in the box. Give your story to another pair of classmates. Read each other's stories.

My Learning Goal

I can read poems and understand rhyme, rhythm, and stanzas.

Poetry

A poem tells thoughts and feelings. Groups of lines in a poem are called **stanzas.** The lines often end with **rhyming words.** Poems often have a pattern of beats called **rhythm.**

Stanza

Rhyming Words

Your Dog

Your dog will always let you know
he loves the beach, the car, the snow.

He loves to fetch and dig and chew,
but what he loves the most is you!

TURN and TALK Read "Your Dog" aloud to hear its rhythm and rhyming words. What is the poem about?

Poetry Anchor Chart

Purpose

To arrange words in a creative way to help readers think or feel

Elements

Rhyme — words with the same ending sound

Rhythm — the pattern of sounds

Repetition — words or lines that repeat

Imagery — words that paint a picture in your mind

Stanza — a group of lines of poetry

Poetry

Preview Vocabulary

Look for these words as you read "Pete at the Zoo," "Keziah," "Rudolph Is Tired of the City," and "Lyle."

lonely	stamp	might	scolding	spread

First Read

Read to understand the text of each poem.

Look at illustrations to help you understand what the poet is describing.

Ask questions about parts you find interesting.

Talk to restate or summarize the poem.

Meet *the* Poet

Gwendolyn Brooks wrote many books of poetry, a novel, and an autobiography. In her poems, she wrote about the daily life and struggles of African Americans. Today, she is known as one of the greatest American poets of all time.

POETRY

By Gwendolyn Brooks

- Pete at the Zoo
- Keziah
- Rudolph Is Tired of the City
- Lyle

AUDIO
Audio with Highlighting

ANNOTATE

Pete at the Zoo

I wonder if the elephant

Is lonely in his stall

When all the boys and girls are gone

And there's no shout at all,

5 And there's no one to stamp before,

No one to note his might.

Does he hunch up, as I do,

Against the dark of night?

CLOSE READ

Explain Patterns and Structures

<u>Underline</u> the words that rhyme in this poem.

lonely without company, alone

stamp to forcefully put a foot down

might power, strength

Keziah

I have a secret place to go.
Not anyone may know.

And sometimes when the wind is rough
I cannot get there fast enough.

5 And sometimes when my mother
Is scolding my big brother,

My secret place, it seems to me,
Is quite the only place to be.

CLOSE READ

Explain Patterns and Structures

Stanzas are groups of lines arranged in a poem or song. Underline the second stanza of this poem.

scolding speaking in an angry way

Vocabulary in Context

You can look for clues to the meaning of a word you don't know in or near the sentence where it appears. Underline the words that help you figure out the meaning of **tend**.

spread stretch out or apart

Rudolph Is Tired of the City

These buildings are too close to me.
I'd like to PUSH away.
I'd like to live in the country.
And spread my arms all day.

5 I'd like to spread my breath out, too—
As farmers' sons and daughters do.

I'd tend the cows and chickens.
I'd do the other chores.
Then, all the hours left I'd go
10 A-SPREADING out-of-doors.

144

Lyle

Tree won't pack his bag and go.
Tree won't go away.
In his first and favorite home
Tree shall stay and stay.

5   Once I liked a little home.
Then I liked another.
I've waved Good-bye to seven homes.
And so have Pops and Mother.

But tree may stay, so stout and straight,
10 And never have to move,
As I, as Pops, as Mother,
From land he learned to love.

CLOSE READ

Monitor Comprehension

Highlight any text that was hard to understand. How can the picture help you understand the poem?

Develop Vocabulary

MY TURN Fill in each blank with a word that has a similar meaning to the word or words below the blank.

lonely	stamp	scolding	spread	might

1. Mom was **scolding** us about the mess.
   talking to

2. The puppy was _____ when its owner left.
   sad

3. The eagle _____ its wings wide.
   opened

4. When Jack is angry, he will _____ his foot
   put down

   with all his _____.
   strength

Check for Understanding

MY TURN Look back at the text to answer the questions. Write the answers.

1. What are some ways you can tell these are poems?

_____

_____

_____

_____

2. Do you think "Pete at the Zoo" is a good title for the first poem? Why or why not?

_____

_____

_____

_____

3. How are the two poems "Rudolph Is Tired of the City" and "Lyle" alike and different?

_____

_____

_____

_____

Explain Patterns and Structures

Rhythm is the pattern of sounds in a poem. It can help poetry sound like music. **Rhyme** is a pattern of words that have the same ending sounds. **Stanzas** are groups of lines that add structure to a poem.

MY TURN Go to the Close Read notes in the poems "Pete at the Zoo" and "Keziah." Underline the pattern or structure of each poem. Explain the patterns and structures you underlined by completing the chart.

Poem	Type of Pattern or Structure I Underlined	How It Helped Me Read the Poem
"Pete at the Zoo"		
"Keziah"		

Monitor Comprehension

When you monitor your comprehension, you check to make sure you understand what you are reading. If you don't understand something, try one of these strategies:

- Go back and read again.

- Look at the pictures.

- Read on to see whether ideas become clearer.

- Ask questions.

MY TURN Go back to the Close Read note in the poem "Lyle." Highlight a part you did not understand. Use what you highlighted to complete the chart.

What I Didn't Understand	What I Did About It	Did It Help?

Reflect and Share

Write to Sources

This week, you read poems that tell how different places affect people. Choose the two poems you liked best. On a separate piece of paper, write an opinion paragraph to tell why you like them.

Give Your Opinion

An opinion paragraph tells how you think or feel.

- Clearly state, or tell, your opinion in the first sentence.

- Give reasons that support your opinion.

- Use words such as **for example** and **so** to connect your opinion and reasons.

Tell which two poems you liked best and why. Use examples from the poem to support your response.

Weekly Question

How do different places make us feel?

I can use language to make connections between reading and writing.

My Learning Goal

Academic Vocabulary

A **suffix** is a word part added to the end of a word. It makes a new word with a new meaning.

quick + **ly**	in a quick way	
	We walked **quickly** to the store.	
nation + **al**	related to the nation	
	The bald eagle is our **national** bird.	

MY TURN Underline the suffix in each new word below. Write what the new word means. On a sheet of paper, use each new word in a sentence.

Word	New Word	Meaning of New Word
different: not the same	differently	
region: an area	regional	

Read Like a Writer, Write for a Reader

Poets choose specific words to make you feel a certain way.

Lines from "Pete at the Zoo"	How I Feel
I wonder if the elephant Is lonely in his stall When all the boys and girls are gone And there's no shout at all,	sad, lonely

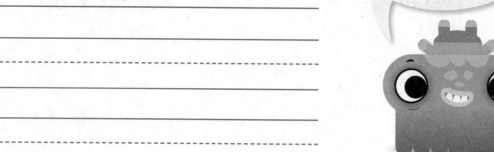 **MY TURN** Write a sentence that makes readers happy. Then write a sentence that makes readers scared. Choose your words carefully.

_____

- -

_____

- -

_____

- -

_____

- -

_____

Poets think about every word.

Spell Words with ch, sh, wh, th, ph, tch

To alphabetize words, say the alphabet to yourself. Write the words in ABC order. If two words start with the same letter, look at the next letters for which comes first.

MY TURN Write the Spelling Words in ABC order. Then write the My Words to Know in ABC order.

1.
brush

2.

3.

4.

5.

6.

7.

8.

9.

10.

My Words to Know

Spelling Words

bunch

patch

what

phone

when

chase

math

brush

thank

dish

My Words to Know

great

before

Sentences and End Punctuation

A sentence begins with a capital letter and ends with a punctuation mark.

Type of Sentence	Example
A **declarative sentence** tells something and ends with a period.	Juan lives in the city.
An **interrogative sentence** asks a question and ends with a question mark.	Has Juan ever lived in the country?
An **exclamatory sentence** expresses strong feeling and ends with an exclamation point.	Juan is the best friend I ever had!

MY TURN Edit this draft. Cross out incorrect end punctuation. Write the correct punctuation above it.

Our city has a zoo? Do you like going to the

zoo. You can see elephants there. They are my

favorite animal? What is your favorite animal?

The zoo opens at 9:00. Is that too early for you.

I can plan, draft, and publish my writing.

End Punctuation and Apostrophes

Authors edit their writing to make it better.

Authors use punctuation after sentences.	Authors use apostrophes in contractions.
I like cats more than dogs. Cats are the best! What pet do you like?	I'm = I am you're = you are he's = he is

MY TURN Edit the paragraph. Fix mistakes in end punctuation and apostrophes. Then edit your writing for end punctuation and apostrophes.

I like to visit the city? There are so many really great things to do. Do you like museums. I like the history museum because its got dinosaur bones. We take the train in. Thats part of the fun.

Revise Drafts by Adding Details

Authors revise their writing to improve it. They add details to sentences to make the writing more interesting. Details give more information.

swinging in a tree

At the zoo, we saw a chimp.

proud

A peacock strutted around.

MY TURN Add words and phrases to make each sentence more interesting. Then revise your own writing by adding details.

We went for a hike.

_____

We saw squirrels.

_____

Revise Drafts by Deleting Words

An author may revise writing by deleting, or taking away, words. An author takes away words or sentences that are not needed or do not make sense.

At the zoo, we saw a ~~tall~~ giraffe. ~~I like giraffes.~~ It was munching leaves from a tree.

MY TURN Revise the draft by deleting words and sentences. Then revise your own writing by deleting words and sentences that are not needed.

I sat by a pond at the zoo. Ducks with bright green feathers swam by me in the water. Ducks can swim as well as fly. Then I saw a frog in the pond. Frogs grow from tadpoles. The frog jumped out onto a rock. It stuck out its tongue from its mouth and snapped up a bug.

Two Different Places

Washington

Washington lies in the northwestern part of the United States.

37
inches

Washington gets about 37 inches of rain in a year.

Washington is home to mountains.

Washington has a rain forest. It gets 12–14 feet of rain each year. In the summer, temperatures are around 60 to 70°F.

Arizona

Arizona lies in the southwestern part of the United States.

8
inches

Arizona gets about 8 inches of rain in a year.

Arizona has a desert. It gets 3–20 inches of rain each year. In the summer, temperatures are above 104°F.

Weekly Question

How can a new place help us change and grow?

TURN and TALK

Look at the information about Washington and Arizona. How are these places alike? How are these places different? How would life be different in each place?

Arizona is home to mountains.

Add and Remove Sounds

SEE and SAY Each sound in a word is a phoneme. You can make new words by adding or removing phonemes. Name the pictures. Listen to the sounds.

What sound, or phoneme, was added to the beginning of the first word to make the second word?

What word can you make when you take away the first sound from the third picture word?

TURN and TALK Work with a partner. Say the name of the first picture. Circle the picture that adds a sound to the beginning. Underline the picture that takes away a sound from the beginning.

Inflected Endings -s, -es, -ed, -ing

MY TURN Some words have endings added to them. Read each base word. Then read the words with their endings. Sometimes the base word changes a little when an ending is added.

boxes = box + -es

Base Word	-s or -es Added	-ed Added	-ing Added
rest	rests	rested	resting
wish	wishes	wished	wishing
drop	drops	dropped	dropping
chase	chases	chased	chasing
copy	copies	copied	copying

TURN and TALK Reread the words with a partner. Which base words changed when an ending was added? How did they change?

Inflected Endings -s, -es, -ed, -ing

Many verbs and nouns have inflected endings. To read a word that ends in **-s**, **-es**, **-ed**, or **-ing**, look for the base word.

MY TURN Read, or decode, each word. Write the base word.

1. hopes   hope

2. mixes _____

3. studies _____

4. grabbed _____

5. taping _____

6. scraped _____

7. switches _____

My Words to Know

MY TURN Read the words in the box and in the sentences. Write a sentence for each word.

follow	form	show

I will **show** you the way. **Form** a line and **follow** me.

1. Follow us home.

2.

3.

TURN and TALK Work with a partner.

- Read one of your sentences, but leave out the new word. Say **blank** instead. For example, "The puppies **blank** their mom."
- Have your partner guess which word belongs in your sentence.
- Take turns until you finish all of your sentences.

My Learning Goal

I can read realistic fiction and understand its plot.

Realistic Fiction

Realistic fiction tells a made-up story that could really happen.

- It has **characters** who act like real people.

- It has a **setting**, or place, where the story occurs.

- It has a **plot**, or story events, that could really happen.

Establish Purpose The purpose for reading realistic fiction is often to enjoy a good story. You may want to find out about a problem the main character has. How does he or she solve the problem?

TURN *and* **TALK** Discuss with a partner your reasons for reading *You Can't Climb a Cactus.* Do you want to find out what the title means? Why is the girl looking up at a cactus? Set your own purpose for reading this text.

REALISTIC FICTION ANCHOR CHART

A realistic fiction story

Has characters who act like real people

Has a beginning, middle, and end

Has a setting that is like real life

Has a plot, or story problem, that could happen

You Can't Climb a Cactus

Preview Vocabulary

Look for these words as you read *You Can't Climb a Cactus.*

excited	favorite	tour	guide	explore

First Read

Look through this text. Make a prediction.

Ask what this text is about.

Read for the purpose you set.

Talk about how this text answers the weekly question.

Meet the Author

Derrick Barnes has written many children's books. He says that reading poems and listening to songs helped him learn to write well. He lives in Charlotte, North Carolina, with his wife Tinka and their four sons: Ezra, Solomon, Silas, and Nnamdi.

You Can't Climb A Cactus

By Derrick Barnes

Illustrated by Steve Cox

AUDIO

Audio with Highlighting

ANNOTATE

excited thrilled; looking forward to

favorite liked better than others

1   Erica was excited about spring vacation.

2   She wanted to visit the new nature center near her home in Seattle.

3   It had plants and bugs, which were two of her favorite things in the world!

CLOSE READ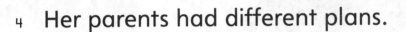

4   Her parents had different plans.

5   "Let's take a trip to Arizona!" Mom said. "We can visit Grandpa Zack."

6   Erica loved Grandpa Zack, but she did not want to visit Arizona.

7   She'd never been there. She knew it would be boring.

Describe and Understand Plot Elements

<u>Underline</u> the words that tell what problem Erica has with her parents' plan.

Make and Confirm Predictions

Highlight the sentence that tells how Erica feels about Arizona. When you first read the story, what prediction did you make about how she will feel by the end of the story?

8 Erica had read a book about Arizona.

9 Compared to Seattle, Arizona seemed strange. It was dry and dusty.

10 Seattle was far from dry. It had lakes and tons of trees.

11 Erica and her dad loved to climb trees.

12 Arizona looked like one big empty desert with weird cactus plants.

13 Erica wasn't sure if Arizona had *any* trees.

14 "You can't climb a cactus!" she said to herself. "The sharp spines would really hurt!"

15 She wished she could stay home.

CLOSE READ

Vocabulary in Context

Look for clues to the meaning of an unfamiliar word in the words around it. <u>Underline</u> the words in the text that tell you what a **vulture** is.

16 As the plane started to land in Arizona, Erica looked out the window.

17 The desert was SO flat.

18 "Look!" she gasped, pointing to a huge bird far off in the sky.

19 "A vulture," said Dad.

20   Grandpa met Erica and her parents at the airport.

21   "I have a surprise for you!" he told Erica, as they walked to his car.

22   From the car window, Erica saw a group of animals. "Look, Grandpa," she said. "Pigs!"

23   "Javelinas," said Grandpa. "They look like wild pigs. But they're a different mammal that lives in the desert."

Make and Confirm Predictions

Highlight the text that helps you understand that Erica will learn something new. When you first read the selection, what prediction did you make about the kind of surprise Grandpa has for Erica?

173

Make and Confirm Predictions

Highlight the sentences that tell what Grandpa's surprise is. Was your prediction correct?

24   Grandpa drove to a tall building. It was made mostly of glass.

25   "This is where I work now!" Grandpa said.

26   Erica read the sign. It said DESERT NATURE CENTER.

27 "Can we go in?" Erica asked.

28 "We sure can," Grandpa said. "I'll sign you up for a tour!"

tour a visit to see things

29 Grandpa handed Erica a guidebook.

30 "It's full of facts about the things you'll see," he said.

guide a person who shows people around

31 Then a guide took Erica and a small group of other children to explore the nature center.

explore to look around a place to learn things

175

32 First, they went inside to see the animals.

33 Lizards scrambled up a glass wall. Scorpions and beetles crawled through the dirt.

34 The tour came to a family of javelinas.

35 "Yay!" squealed Erica as two baby javelinas scurried by. It was so cool to see them up close!

36 Next, the tour went outside.

37 They walked near a stream lined with colorful wildflowers.

38 Erica tried to match the flowers with the pictures in her book.

39 Then the guide's phone rang.

40 "Please excuse me," she said, as she walked away.

Describe and Understand Plot Elements

Underline the sentence that shows Erica was interested in what she saw.

41 While the guide was gone, Erica took over the tour!

42 She used her guidebook to share fun facts about the plants.

43 The other children loved learning from someone their own age.

44 When the guide returned, she let Erica finish leading the tour.

45 "You should be a guide," she told her. "Why don't you be my assistant?"

CLOSE READ

46   The guide invited Erica back.

47   For the rest of the week, Erica went to work with Grandpa Zack.

48   While Grandpa did his job, she helped with the tours.

49   When it was time to go home to Seattle, the guide gave Erica a gift. It was a little cactus plant.

Describe and Understand Plot Elements

Underline the text that tells what Erica did during her week in Arizona.

50 Back home, Erica missed Arizona.

51 She decided to make an Arizona corner in her room.

52 She hung photos from the trip.

53 Then she put the cactus on a little table.

54 Erica loved to look at her cactus.

55 It always reminded her of Arizona and the best vacation ever.

56 "It's true you can't climb a cactus," she thought. "You sure can love one, though!"

Describe and Understand Plot Elements

Erica was unhappy about going to Arizona at first. Underline the text that shows she solved her problem.

Develop Vocabulary

MY TURN Use a dictionary to find the meanings and pronunciations of these words from *You Can't Climb a Cactus*. With a partner, take turns saying aloud each word. Write the meanings in your own words. Then use the dictionary to find a related word. The first one is done for you.

Word	Meaning	Related Word
excited	thrilled; looking forward to	excitement
favorite		
tour		
guide		
explore		

Check for Understanding

MY TURN Look back at the text to answer the questions. Write the answers.

1. Could this story happen in real life? Why or why not?

_____

_____

_____

2. How does the dialogue help you understand the story?

_____

_____

_____

3. What does Erica know that helps her become a guide in the nature center?

_____

_____

_____

Describe and Understand Plot Elements

Look for these plot elements in a story:

- **Events** that happen in time order.

- A **conflict,** or **problem,** for the main character.

- A **resolution** at the end. Usually, the main character solves the problem.

MY TURN Read the text again independently. Then go to the Close Read notes. Underline plot elements. Then complete the chart to describe the story's events, problem, and resolution.

What are the main events in the story?

What is Erica's conflict?

What is the resolution?

Make and Confirm Predictions

When you make a prediction, you combine what you know with clues in the text to guess what will happen. When story events match what you thought, you confirm your prediction. Correct your prediction if events do not match what you thought.

You can use what you know about the genre to make predictions. You know stories have a conflict that is resolved. You can predict that the conflict of the character in this story will be solved.

MY TURN Go back to the Close Read notes. Use your predictions and the evidence you highlighted to complete the chart.

Text I highlighted	I predicted . . .	Now I know . . .
Arizona seemed strange.		Erica LOVED Arizona.

Reflect and Share

Talk About It

Have you ever gone to a new place that surprised you? In what way were you surprised? How did the place help you change and grow? Use examples from the texts to support your response.

Connect with events you read about in stories.

Listen and Build on Ideas

When having a discussion, it is important to listen and to share.

- Make sure everyone gets a chance to talk.

- Build on the ideas of others.

Use these sentence starters to help you.

Can you tell me more about . . .
I like the idea that . . .

Weekly Question

How can a new place help us change and grow?

I can use language to make connections between reading and writing.

Academic Vocabulary

different	difference	compare	comparison
affect	region	locate	location

MY TURN Read the related words in the chart above. Now look back through the pages of the unit and at the Word Wall. Write other words that you have learned on the lines below.

_____

_____

_____

_____

_____

_____

_____

_____

TURN and TALK Use the words in the chart and the words you wrote to discuss the Essential Question: **How do different places affect us?**

Read Like a Writer, Write for a Reader

Authors often include pictures to help you understand the information in the text. Pictures can also add information not found in the words.

Text and Picture	What I Learn from the Picture
"Lizards scrambled up a glass wall."	I can see what a lizard looks like.

MY TURN Write a sentence about an animal you like. Draw a picture to help your readers understand.

_____

- -

_____

Spell Words with -s, -es, -ed, -ing

Notice the spelling changes in the Spelling Words when you add endings. Final consonants are often doubled when the base word ends in a VC pattern.

MY TURN Sort the Spelling Words by the endings that were added. Then write the My Words to Know.

-s

notes

-ed

-es

-ing

My Words to Know

Spelling Words

babies
boxes
dropped
dropping
lunches
notes
smiled
switches
taking
tunes

My Words to Know

follow
show

Use Resources to Spell Words

Use a dictionary to find correct spellings. If a word changes when **-s, -es, -ed,** or **-ing** is added, it is shown in the dictionary entry.

grin (GRIN), *VERB*. to smile. **grins, grinned, grinning**

hope (HOHP) *VERB*. to want something to happen. **hopes, hoped, hoping**

hurry (HER ee) *VERB*. to move quickly. **hurries, hurried, hurrying**

joke (JOHK) *VERB*. to say something funny. **jokes, joked, joking**

MY TURN Edit this draft. Cross out each word that is spelled incorrectly. Look it up in the dictionary, and write it correctly above the word.

hurries

My friend Jayden ~~hurryes~~ to get ready for school.

He jokees that I am always late. Today I hurryed to

get ready. I hoped to be on time, and I was. Jayden

grined. "I won't be jokeing today," he said.

My Learning Goal

I can plan, draft, and publish my writing.

Peer Edit

Peer editing means sharing your work with classmates.

When you peer edit a classmate's work, you give feedback to help the writer improve what he or she wrote. You should:

- Start by saying something good about the writer's work. For example, say: I like the way you _____.

- Tell the writer a clear idea to make the writing better. For example, say:
  If you added more details about the setting, I could picture it better.

- Ask the writer questions to clarify details. For example, say:
  What color is the bike in your story?

 **MY TURN** Choose a piece of your writing. Ask a classmate to peer edit your writing.

How to Write a Final Draft

Authors revise their work before they write a final draft.

To write a final draft:

1. Use feedback you received to revise your draft.

2. Read your work out loud.

3. Make other changes, if needed.

4. Check spelling, grammar, and punctuation.

5. Make changes, if needed.

6. Read your final draft one more time. Make sure it's something you'll want to share with an audience.

Publish and Celebrate

There are many ways to publish your writing: in print, on a computer, or aloud in front of an audience.

Here are some tips to follow when you publish your writing on paper:

☐ Write your final draft neatly or type it on a computer.

☐ Keep margins (white space at the top and bottom and sides). Include a picture.

Here are some tips to follow when you read your writing aloud to an audience:

☐ Speak clearly and loudly enough to be heard (but not too loud!).

☐ Read at a normal pace (not too fast, not too slow).

☐ Look at your listeners now and then.

☐ Present a picture or other visual. Hold it so that all can see.

UNIT THEME

You Are Here

TURN and TALK

Connect to the Question
With your partner, look back at each text. Write one location from each and tell how it makes you feel. Discuss why the place affects you that way. Use this information to help you answer the Essential Question.

WEEK **3**

Places We Go

Location	Feeling

BOOK CLUB

WEEK **2**

Maybe Something Beautiful

Location	Feeling

BOOK CLUB

WEEK **1**

How Many Stars in the Sky?

Location	Feeling

Poetry

Location	Feeling

WEEK 4

WEEK 6

WEEK 5

You Can't Climb a Cactus

Location	Feeling

BOOK CLUB

Essential Question

MY TURN

In your notebook, answer the Essential Question: How do different places affect us?

WEEK 6 Project

Now it is time to apply what you learned about places in your **WEEK 6 PROJECT: The Best Place!**

r-Controlled Vowels ar, or, ore, oar

When the letter **r** comes after a vowel or vowel team, the vowel has a different sound. These letter groups are called **r-controlled vowels**.

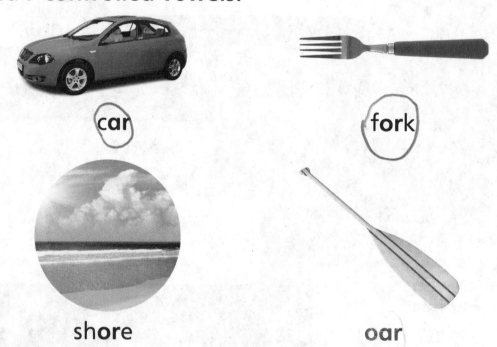

car

fork

shore

oar

MY TURN Read, or decode, these words.

star	born	core	soar
spark	thorn	chore	board
carpet	forty	before	roaring

TURN and TALK Reread the words in the chart with a partner. <u>Underline</u> the **r-controlled** vowel groups in each word.

r-Controlled Vowels ar, or, ore, oar

MY TURN Write a word from the box to name each picture. Then read each word you wrote.

board	corn	horse
store	shark	garden

corn

_____

_____

_____

_____

_____

My Words to Know

MY TURN Find and <u>underline</u> the boxed words in the story. Then read the story.

also	large	small

Dad made a <u>large</u> pizza for him and a small pizza for me. He also made a large salad for both of us. Yum!

Use the boxed words to complete the sentences.

1. A hippo is a _____ animal.

2. An ant is a _____ insect.

3. Jen is a girl, and Kate is _____ a girl.

TURN and TALK Answer these questions with a partner.

1. What are some other **large** animals?

2. What are some other **small** insects?

3. What do you have that your partner **also** has?

Spell Words with ar, or, ore, oar

When **r** comes after a vowel, the vowel sounds different.

MY TURN Sort the Spelling Words by their **r**-controlled vowels. Then write My Words to Know.

ar

cart

ore

or

oar

My Words to Know

Spelling Words

core

cart

tore

fort

chore

board

mark

roar

garden

forest

My Words to Know

also

large

The BEST Place

Activity

Your community is having a contest to choose the best place in town. Write a persuasive paragraph telling why your favorite place should win.

Let's Read!

This week you will read three texts about places in a community. Today's article gives information about a museum.

1 Exploring Museums

2 Save Our Movie Theater

3 The Wonders of the Grand Canyon

Generate Questions

 **COLLABORATE** With a partner, choose a place you think is the best place in town. To generate questions for inquiry, list what you want to know and what you need to research.

Use Academic Words

COLLABORATE The picture shows one place in a community. With a partner, talk about a place in the community that you like. Respond using the academic vocabulary you learned in the unit. Be sure to use these words in your paragraph.

Academic Vocabulary

affect	location
compare	region
different	

Favorite Place Research Plan

Follow this research plan with help from your teacher.

Day 1 Think of questions for research.

Day 2 Conduct an interview with someone who knows the place well.

Day 3 Write a persuasive paragraph for the contest.

Day 4 Revise and edit your paragraph.

Day 5 Present your paragraph to your classmates.

What Do YOU Think?

People write persuasive paragraphs to convince, or persuade, someone to think or do something. A persuasive text includes these characteristics:

- the author's **argument.** This is the main idea that the author wants you to agree with.

- **reasons** the author gives to support the argument and persuade you.

COLLABORATE With a partner, read "Save Our Movie Theater." Then fill in the chart.

Author's argument

Author's reasons to support the argument

What the author is trying to persuade the reader to think or do

Interview an Expert

Think of someone who knows a lot about your chosen place in the community. It may be someone who works there or has lived in the community for a long time.

Ask the person questions about the place. Be sure to plan your questions before the interview.

Ask each question clearly and allow time for the person to answer. You can take notes or record the person's answers.

MY TURN Questions I want to ask an expert to learn facts or details about my favorite place:

1. _____

2. _____

COLLABORATE How will you find an expert on your location? Who might it be?

_____

_____

Persuasive Paragraph

Writers use persuasive words to get the reader to think or do something.

Argument

Reasons

The art museum is the best place in town! Everyone must visit it. You will see all kinds of beautiful artwork there. You can learn about artists and how they made their art. There is even a kids' room where kids can have fun making their own art. If you have not been to the art museum, you are missing out! Everyone knows it is the best place in town.

Persuasive Words

Primary or Secondary?

COLLABORATE You can use relevant primary and secondary sources to learn more about your favorite place. Your interview is a primary source you can use.

Primary Sources	Secondary Sources
• made by someone who is or was there	• made by someone who got information from other sources
Examples interviews photos or videos diaries letters maps	**Examples** books magazine articles encyclopedias many Web sites

Relevant sources are sources that will make your project better. They are only relevant if they are about your topic and add useful information.

COLLABORATE With a partner, identify a relevant primary source and secondary source to learn more about your favorite place. Gather your sources.

Include Media

Media can be audio, photos, drawings, maps, and other visuals. When you gather sources, identify and include only relevant, or useful, sources that will make your writing interesting and answer questions a reader might have. If you choose carefully, media can help you persuade readers to agree with your opinion.

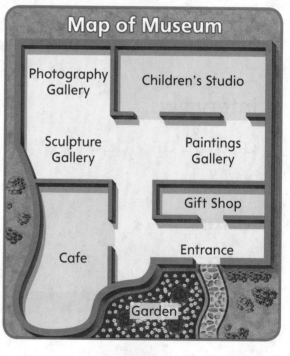

COLLABORATE With a partner, talk about the photos and map. Will this information help persuade a reader to visit the art museum? Then, choose a photo, a diagram, a map, or other relevant media source to use with your presentation.

Revise

COLLABORATE When you revise a persuasive paragraph, make sure you clearly state your opinion and include reasons that support it. Does your paragraph convince readers to agree with you? Look for places to add persuasive words and phrases to make your position more convincing.

Should you add one of these?

You need to	Everyone knows
You should	Everyone agrees
You must	It is important that

Edit

COLLABORATE Read your persuasive paragraph again. This time be sure you used correct conventions.

Check your paragraph to be sure

☐ you spelled words correctly

☐ you wrote complete sentences

☐ your sentences end with a period or question mark

Share

 **COLLABORATE** Read your persuasive paragraph to a small group. Imagine they are the contest judges. Use a lively voice to convince them to agree with your choice for the best place in town.

- Speak clearly at an appropriate pace. Do not speak too fast or too slow.

- Follow the conventions of language. Use complete sentences.

- Listen actively when another speaker takes a turn. Look at the speaker and pay attention.

Reflect

MY TURN Complete the sentences.

In my persuasive paragraph, I think I did a good job of

_____

_____

Something I will change next time is

_____

_____

Reflect on Your Goals

Look back at your unit goals at the beginning of this unit. Use a different color to rate yourself again.

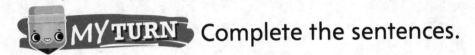 **MY TURN** Complete the sentences.

Reflect on Your Reading

My favorite selection in the unit is

_____

_____

_____

Reflect on Your Writing

My best writing from this unit is

_____

_____

_____

Nature's Wonders

Essential Question

What patterns do we see in nature?

▶ Watch

"Patterns Around Us" A **pattern** is the way colors or shapes appear over and over in a certain order. What do you notice about patterns in nature?

TURN and **TALK** What patterns did you see?

SAVVAS
realize™
Go ONLINE for all lessons.

▶ VIDEO

🔊 AUDIO

🎮 GAME

✏ ANNOTATE

📖 BOOK

🔍 RESEARCH

Reading Workshop

Reading-Writing Bridge

- Academic Vocabulary
- Read Like a Writer, Write for a Reader
- Spelling • Language and Conventions

Writing Workshop

Informational Text

- Introduce and Immerse
- Develop Elements • Develop Structure
- Writer's Craft • Publish, Celebrate, and Assess

Project-Based Inquiry

- Inquire • Research • Collaborate

Independent Reading

Reading independently helps you become a better reader. On the next page, keep track of your independent reading.

Follow these steps to help you set a purpose for reading on your own.

1. Ask yourself if you are reading to have fun, to learn, or to read something by your favorite author.

2. Select a book that helps you meet that main purpose. Skim through the pages. Look at the images. Ask yourself questions like these:

   - Who is this person?
   - What is this thing?
   - What is happening?
   - Where is this place?

Look for the answers to your questions as you read.

My Reading Log

Date	Book	Pages Read	Minutes Read	My Ratings
				☺ 😐 ☹
				☺ 😐 ☹
				☺ 😐 ☹
				☺ 😐 ☹
				☺ 😐 ☹
				☺ 😐 ☹

Unit Goals

In this unit, you will

- read informational texts
- write a fact sheet
- learn about patterns in nature

 **Color** the pictures to answer.

I know about informational text and understand its features and structures.	👍	👎
I can learn and use words to read and write informational text.	👍	👎
I can use elements of informational text to write a list article.	👍	👎
I can talk with others about what patterns we see in nature.	👍	👎

Academic Vocabulary

behavior	evidence	identify	similar	design

In this unit you will read about patterns in nature. You will **identify** patterns in the appearance and **behavior** of animals and plants. You will also see **evidence** that the **design** of a pattern on an animal or plant helps protect it. Using patterns is one way that animals and plants are **similar**.

TURN and TALK Use the Academic Vocabulary words to talk with your partner about patterns in nature. What patterns in nature do you see in the pictures?

See How They Grow

LEAVES

STEM
THE CELERY!

A vegetable is part of a plant. Which part? That depends on the kind of vegetable.

LEAVES

LEAVES

LEAVES

ROOT

ROOT

ROOT

ROOT
THE CARROT!

Some vegetables hide from sight. They are roots underground. A carrot is a plant's root.

Some vegetables are the stems, or stalks, of plants. Celery is the stem of a plant. So is asparagus.

LEAVES
THE LETTUCE!

ROOT

Some vegetables are the leaves of a plant. Leafy vegetables include lettuce, spinach, and kale.

Weekly Question

What patterns can we notice in a garden?

Quick Write What do you know about the parts of plants? What can you learn about vegetable plants from the diagram?

Add and Remove Sounds

SEE and SAY You can recognize and make new words by adding or removing sounds, or phonemes. Name the pictures. Listen to the sounds.

What sound, or phoneme, do you add to the end of the first word to make the second word?

What sound, or phoneme, do you take away from the end of the first word to make the second word?

TURN and TALK Work with a partner. Say the name of the first picture. <u>Underline</u> the picture that adds a sound to the end.

Contractions

A **contraction** is a word that you make when you put two words together. You drop one or more letters and put an apostrophe in place of the missing letter or letters.

do + not = don't

MY TURN Read each pair of words. Then read, or decode, the contraction by putting the words together.

Contractions with not		Contractions with will	
is not	isn't	I will	I'll
have not	haven't	he will	he'll
did not	didn't	she will	she'll
would not	wouldn't	they will	they'll

TURN and TALK Reread the words with a partner. Look to see what happens to **not** and **will** when each word is joined to another word. Then read these contractions. What two words make up each contraction? In which of the lists does each contraction belong?

don't   you'll

Contractions

 Write a contraction by putting the two words together.

1. are not   aren't

2. should not

3. we will

4. you will

Decode, or read, these contractions. Write the two words that make up each contraction.

5. I'll

6. isn't

7. they'll

My Words to Know

MY TURN Some words are used often. These words are called high-frequency words. You will have to remember these words. Often, you can't sound them out.

Find the <u>underlined</u> words in the sentences. Write them on the lines. Then read the words.

There are many <u>different</u> kinds of apples.
I am standing <u>between</u> Rob and Julia.
The teacher split the class into two <u>even</u> groups.

1. _____

2. _____

3. _____

TURN and TALK Work with a partner. Write these words in a list: **different**, **between**, **even**. Read the words to each other several times.

My Learning Goal

I can read informational text and understand text structure.

Informational Text

Text structures are ways of organizing ideas. Here are two informational text structures.

- **Chronological,** or time order, text structure puts events or steps in the order in which they happen.

- **Cause-and-effect** text structure tells what happens and why it happens.

TURN and TALK Tell about a book or article you have read that told you how to do something. What did you learn to do? How did the steps help you? What text structure did the text have?

When I give steps, I begin with the word "First."

Informational Text Anchor Chart

Purpose

To explain a topic or to give facts and details about people, places, events, or ideas

Text Structures

Chronological
puts details in time order.

Description
tells details about a topic to explain it.

Cause and Effect
tells what happens and why it happens.

Problem and Solution
explains a problem and shows how it is solved.

A Green Kid's Guide to Watering Plants

Preview Vocabulary

Look for these words as you read *A Green Kid's Guide to Watering Plants*.

| arrange | certain | moist | soggy | place |

First Read

Look at the title and pictures to decide what this text is about.

Ask questions about the topic before you read.

Read to see if the text answers your questions.

Talk about what you found interesting.

Meet the illustrator

Laura Zarrin spent a lot of time outdoors as a child. She saw nature up close as she explored creeks and climbed trees. She uses that knowledge to create art for many books.

A Green Kid's Guide to
Watering Plants

by Richard Lay
illustrated by Laura Zarrin

AUDIO

Audio with
Highlighting

ANNOTATE

225

Vocabulary in Context

Authors will sometimes tell you what a word means in the same sentence. Underline the meaning of **gardeners**.

arrange to put in a neat or specific way

Are You Ready to Plant?

1 Gardeners are people who grow plants. "Being green" means learning how to live on Earth without hurting it.

2 You have been working hard to be a green gardener. You've built your raised bed and made compost. And, you've fertilized your soil. Now, it is time to plant and water your fruits and vegetables!

3 Green gardeners understand that plants need water. But, they do not waste it. Green gardeners learn how to arrange their plants to conserve water.

Study, Study, Study

4   A green gardener learns about plants before planting them. Different plants have different needs. Some plants need a lot of water to grow. Others need little water.

5   A green gardener also learns about the weather where he or she lives. Some places get a lot of rain. Others get little rain and a lot of sun. Some areas have soil that won't grow certain plants.

6   A green gardener grows only what is best for his or her area. Study what will grow best in your area. Then, make a list of what plants to put in your raised bed.

CLOSE READ

Ask and Answer Questions

Highlight a text detail on this page that you can generate, or ask, a question about.

certain particular; some

Where to Plant?

7   When you were studying, you probably noticed that plants need different amounts of water. Plants that grow on vines, such as cucumbers, need less water. Other plants, like beans, need more water.

8   A green gardener can conserve water by planting in groups. Grow vegetables with vines together. Grow beans in another part of the garden. Then you will not waste water on plants that may not need it.

9   Another way to conserve water is to grow plants in squares instead of rows. When the plants are older, their leaves touch each other. This makes a covering over the bed and reduces evaporation.

Identify Text Structure

This text tells what to do first, next, and last. <u>Underline</u> the word **First**. Then <u>underline</u> the words that tell you what to do first.

moist slightly wet

soggy very wet, soaked

It's Time to Plant!

10 To plant seeds or seedlings, first smooth the soil with a rake. Remove any rocks, sticks, or trash. Cover the soil with compost. Then water it to make it moist, but not soggy.

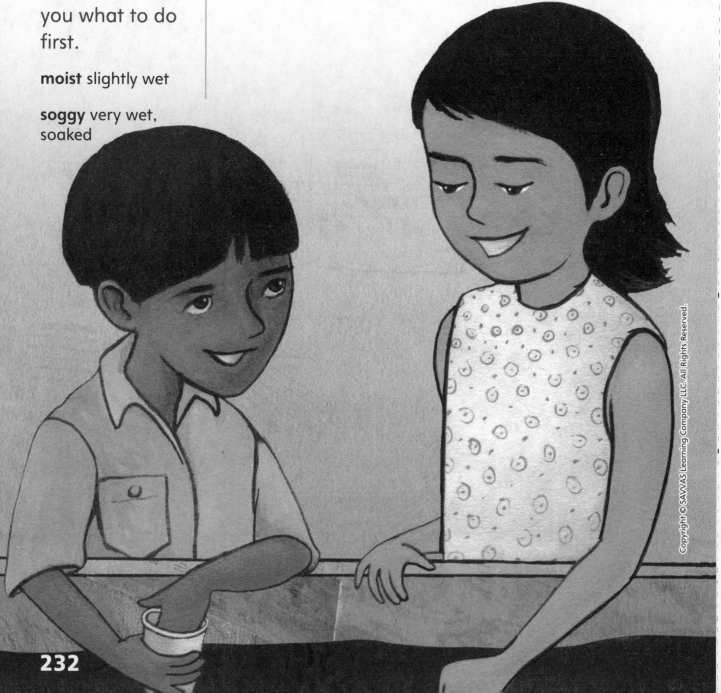

11 To plant seeds, take a small stick and make rows. Make holes the right depth for the seeds. Larger seeds should be down about one inch (3 cm). Smaller seeds should stay at the top of the soil.

12 It is best to put two or more seeds in each hole. That way you can be sure to get plants in every hole.

13 Finally, after planting the seeds or seedlings, check the soil. Do not let it dry out. Green gardeners keep soil moist.

Identify Text Structure

Underline the word **Finally**. It tells what to do last. Then <u>underline</u> the last thing you should do when you plant seeds or seedlings.

Are They Thirsty?

14 Your seeds are planted and shoots are coming up. A green gardener checks the soil every day to see if the plants need water.

15 Plants use their roots to drink. Roots have little hairs that take water from the ground. Then the water is sent to the rest of the plant. So, plants can only get water that is underground.

16 Some gardeners use too much water. They waste it. This is a problem. Our planet has little water to use for people and plants.

17 Green gardeners understand that plants need water. But, they do not waste it. Green gardeners conserve water.

Identify Text Structure

Underline the words that tell what causes water to go to the roots.

Plants Hate Showers

18 Some gardeners make a big mistake. They give their plants showers. They use sprinklers in the garden. But plants hate showers. They love baths.

19 Sprinklers put most of the water on the leaves. But, plants cannot get water through the leaves. They can only get water from the roots.

20 One of the best ways to get water to the roots is to use soaker hoses. These are water hoses with little holes in them. When you turn on the faucet, water slowly drips into the ground. Water then goes to the roots.

place put or set

21 Some gardeners place their soaker hoses near where the plant goes into the ground. To use less water, green gardeners bury their soaker hoses. That way, the water comes out by the roots.

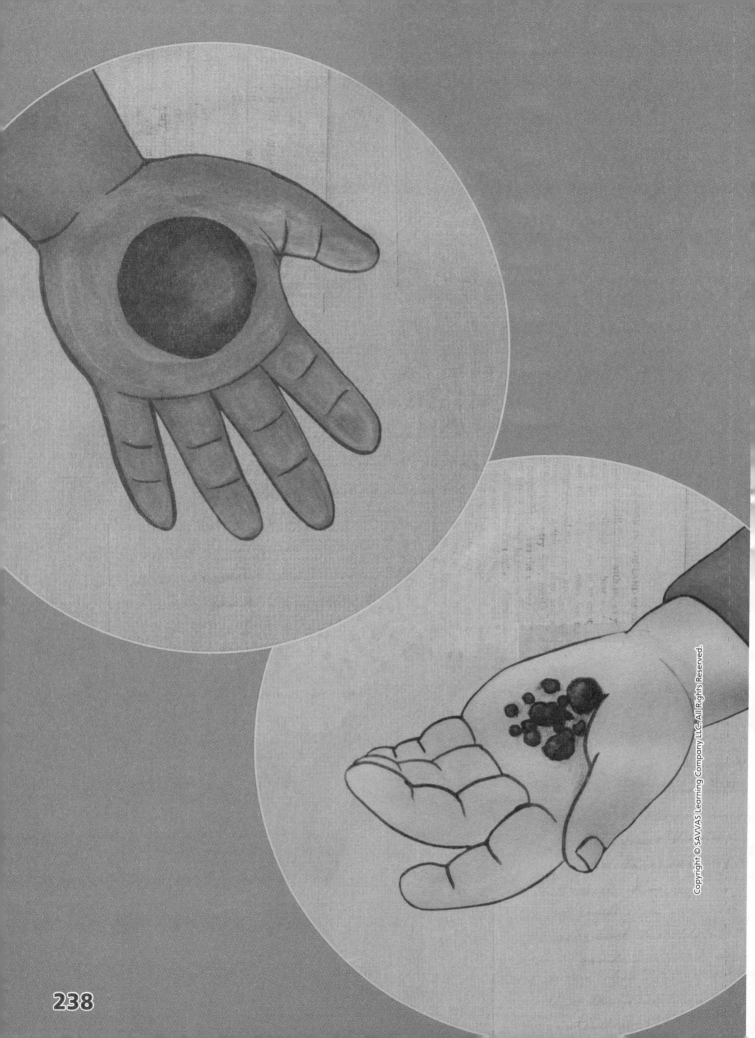

When to Give Your Plants a Drink

22 To check the soil, pick up a handful of dirt and squeeze it. If you can make a ball, do not add water. If you cannot make a ball, your soil is dry. It is time to water your plants.

23 Green gardeners water in the morning. This is when the air is cooler. So, more water gets into the ground. And, they use less water.

24 The amount of time you water depends on your plants and soil. After watering for a while, dig down 12 inches (30 cm) in the raised bed. If the bottom of the hole is damp, you have watered enough.

Stop Losing Water

25 The sun can evaporate water in the ground. It makes water hot and changes it into a gas. The gas then rises. Because of this, soil loses water.

26 Soil with no covering loses a lot of water. A green gardener conserves water by making a covering for the soil. You can cover the garden's soil with compost.

27 Another covering for your garden is mulch. Straw is good mulch. Old newspapers can be mulch. Both will help keep water in the soil.

28 It is important to cover soil in the fall and winter. A good covering for this time of the year is winter rye grass. It will also give plants food in the spring.

Vocabulary in Context

Other words in the text can help you understand a new word. Underline the words that help you understand the meaning of **mulch**.

242

Harvest the Rain

29   A green gardener can also conserve water by saving rain. During the summer it may not rain very much. This is not a problem. With an adult's help you can collect rain by making a rain barrel.

30   A green gardener uses the water in the rain barrel to reduce the water taken from Earth. And, this water is free of chemicals that may hurt his or her plants.

31   You need water. Plants need water. But a green gardener does not waste water. A green gardener conserves it!

Ask and Answer Questions

Highlight a text detail that you might understand in a deeper way if you ask a question about it.

Develop Vocabulary

MY TURN Fill in each blank with a word that has a similar meaning to the word or words below it.

arrange	certain	moist	soggy	place

1. We put too much water on the seeds. Now the soil is

   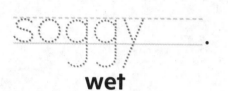 .

   wet

2. Please _____ two seeds into each hole.

   put

3. We will _____ the plants in neat rows.

   put in order

4. The dirt was _____ after the rain shower.

   damp

5. We plant seeds at _____ times of the year.

   special

Check for Understanding

MY TURN Write the answers to the questions. Look back at the text to answer the questions.

1. How can you tell this is an informational text?

Sturniolo triplets ✗ᵞᵞ$

2. Why do you think the author used section headings like "Are You Ready to Plant?" and "Study, Study, Study"?

3. Why is it important to be a green gardener when you water your plants?

Identify Text Structure

One characteristic of informational text is its text structure. A list of **steps in a process**, in which a writer tells how to do something in steps, is a **chronological** text structure.

MY TURN Go to the Close Read notes in "It's Time to Plant!" Follow the directions to underline words that tell chronological order. Use the parts you underlined and other text evidence to complete the chart.

Time Order	Steps for Planting a Garden
First	
Next	**Remove rocks, sticks, or trash.**
Then	
Then	**Water the soil.**
Next	**Make rows and small holes.**
Then	
Finally	

Ask and Answer Questions

Asking, or generating, questions before, during, and after reading helps you understand the text in a deeper way. It also helps you learn information.

MY TURN Go back to the Close Read notes. Highlight details you have questions about. Use what you highlighted to write questions in the chart. Use text evidence to write an answer to each question.

Questions	Answers
you	

Reflect and Share

Talk About It

Look back at what you read this week about plants and places. What information about your area would help you choose which plants to grow? Use evidence from the text in your response.

Make Comments to Show Agreement

In a discussion, it is important to let others know when you agree with their ideas.

- Wait for your turn to speak.

- Speak when you are recognized, or called on.

- Build on others' ideas.

Use these sentence starters to help you agree and disagree respectfully.

I agree with you that . . .
I agree, and I also think that . . .

Weekly Question

What patterns can we notice in a garden?

I can use language to make connections between reading and writing informational texts.

My Learning Goal

Academic Vocabulary

Related words are words that are connected in some way. They can share word parts. They can have almost the same meaning or an opposite meaning.

MY TURN For each vocabulary word, write a word that is related to it in some way. Then share your words with the class or add them to the Word Wall.

Word	Related Word	How It Is Related
behavior	behave	It shares a word part.
evidence	proof	
identify	identification	
similar		
design		

Read Like a Writer, Write for a Reader

Authors organize their ideas to help readers understand a text. When authors write about how to do something, they use words that show the order of the steps. This is called chronological order.

Steps in Order	How the Text Structure Helps
To plant seeds or seedlings, first smooth the soil with a rake. Remove any rocks, sticks, or trash. Cover the soil with compost. Then water it to make it moist, but not soggy. . . . Finally, after planting the seeds or seedlings, check the soil.	Reading the steps helps me know the order in which to do things. If the steps were not in order, I would not know how to plant seeds the right way.

MY TURN Write steps to tell how to do something. Use words such as **first**, **then**, and **last**.

_____

- -

_____

- -

_____

- -

_____

Spell Contractions

In contractions, two words are joined together to make one word. One of the two words is shortened.

MY TURN Sort the Spelling Words by the word that is shortened. Then write the My Words to Know.

is
he's

not

will

are

Spelling Words

you'll
I'll
he's
isn't
wasn't
she's
don't
what's
we're
you're

My Words to Know

different
between

My Words to Know

Singular and Plural Nouns

A **singular noun** names one person, place, animal, or thing. A **plural noun** names more than one.

Rule	Singular	Plural
Add **-s** to most nouns to name more than one.	cat flower	cats flowers
Add **-es** to nouns that end in **x**, **ch**, **sh**, **s**, or **ss**.	fox bench dish bus dress	foxes benches dishes buses dresses

MY TURN Edit this draft. Fix incorrect spellings of plural nouns. The first one is done for you.

Two ~~class~~ classes at my school planted a garden. We filled four large wood boxs with soil. Then we made holes two inchs apart in the soil. We put a seed in each hole. Many shootes grew out of the soil. I hope they will all grow into big plantes.

I can use elements of informational text to write a list article.

My Learning Goal

List Article

In a list article, an author picks a topic and writes a main idea that gives more information on the topic. The author lists details to support the main idea.

Kinds of Animals •———— **Topic**

There are many different kinds of animals. •—— **Introduction**
Scientists sort animals into groups, including
mammals, birds, and reptiles, based on features
they share. •———————————————————— **Main Idea**

1. Mammals have fur or hair. They feed their babies milk.
2. Birds have feathers. Their feathers keep •—— **Details** them warm and help them fly.
3. Reptiles have scales. Their scales help protect their bodies.

Graphic

Mammals, birds, and reptiles are three groups of animals. The animals in each group are alike in certain ways. •—— **Conclusion**

Generate Ideas

An author brainstorms, or thinks of ideas, before beginning to write.

MY TURN Plan a first draft of your list article. Generate ideas by thinking of three topics you could write about.

Topics

Use this checklist to help decide which topic to use:

☐ This topic will be interesting to my readers.

☐ I can find interesting details about this topic.

☐ I will enjoy writing about this topic.

Plan Your List Article

Authors organize ideas to plan what they will write.

MY TURN Decide on a topic for your list article. List the items you want to write about. Be sure to number them in order. Write details with information about each item. Then share your ideas in Writing Club. Listen to what others say about your ideas.

Topic:	
Items	**Details**

GRASSY Places

The places in these pictures have lots of grass and few trees. They have cold winters and hot summers.

The **prairie** in North America is called . . .

a **steppe** in Europe and Asia.

a **veldt** in some parts of Africa.

the **pampas** in South America.

Grasses

Prairies have mostly grasses and not many trees.

Prairie grasses can grow very tall.

Animals

Prairie dogs, owls, hawks, rabbits, and coyotes live on prairies in the United States. So do grasshoppers and flies.

Prairie dogs live underground.

Weekly Question

What patterns can we see on a prairie?

Quick Write Look at the four pictures on the map. How are these places alike? Write your ideas below.

Recognize Changes in Words

 **SEE and SAY** You can recognize new words made by changing the middle phoneme, or sound, in a word. Say the names of the pictures.

What middle phoneme, or sound, changed from the first picture to the second?

 **TURN and TALK** Work with a partner. Name the pictures. Say what sound changed.

Long a: ai, ay, ea

The vowel teams, or digraphs, **ai**, **ay**, and **ea** can make the long **a** sound. Sometimes, when two vowels are together in a syllable, the first vowel is long and the second one is silent, as in the teams **ai** and **ay**. Sometimes, the vowel team **ea** makes the long **a** sound.

MY TURN Decode, or read, the words below and listen for the vowel-team sound in each word.

ai	ay	ea
sn<u>ai</u>l	pay	break
paint	Sunday	great
brain	Monday	steak

TURN and TALK Reread the words in the chart with a partner. <u>Underline</u> the vowel team in each word that makes the long **a** sound. Then choose two of the words and use them in sentences. Share your sentences with your partner.

Long a: ai, ay, ea

MY TURN Decode, or read, the words in the box. Then use the words to complete the sentences.

crayon	Friday	main
brain	break	great

1. My sister likes to draw with a blue crayon.

2. On _____ we took a _____ from the ball game to have lunch.

3. In science, we learned about the _____ and other parts of the body.

4. The _____ idea in the book is that dogs are _____.

My Words to Know

MY TURN Read the words in the box. Then write a sentence using each word.

kind	change	air

a b c d e

f g

Damaris Tapia

TURN and TALK Read your sentences aloud with a partner. Talk about the sentences, and make any corrections needed.

My Learning Goal

I can read informational text and use its text features.

Spotlight on Genre

Informational Text

Informational text tells **facts** about a topic. It includes **main**, or **central**, **ideas** about the topic and important **details**. Informational text may also include:

- **text features and graphics**, such as headings, photos, captions, labels, and bold words
- a **glossary** and an **index**

TURN and TALK

Describe a book or article you have read about an animal. What made the text informational? What kinds of text features did it include?

Photos in a text are a clue that it has real information.

Informational Text Anchor Chart

 Purpose
- To give information about a topic

 Text Structure
- Descriptive
- Compare and contrast
- Problem and solution

 Text Features
- Headings
- Bold words
- Photos
- Captions
- Glossary
- Index

A Home on the Prairie

Preview Vocabulary

Look for these words as you read *A Home on the Prairie*.

prairie	habitat	grazers	burrows	colonies

First Read

Look through this text. Make a prediction using the text features.

Read to see whether the text matches your prediction.

Ask questions to clarify information.

Talk about the text with a partner.

Meet *the* Author

David C. Lion loves to go out on his boat and fish. He lives in Glens Falls, New York, with his wife Kathy and their cat Jeep. He has also written a book called *A Home in the Swamp*.

A Home on the Prairie

by David C. Lion

 AUDIO

Audio with Highlighting

 ANNOTATE

What Is This Place?

1   Just imagine you're surrounded by tall grass. When you look up, you see nothing but sky.

2   You hear a rattlesnake shake its tail. You watch a prairie dog dive into a hole.

3   Where are we?

A rattlesnake shakes its tail to warn its enemies.

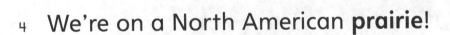

Prairies have very few trees.

CLOSE READ

Confirm or Adjust Predictions

Highlight a bold word that helped you predict the topic of this text.

4   We're on a North American **prairie**!

5   A prairie is a type of **habitat**. A habitat is where a plant or animal usually lives.

6   A prairie is a large, open grassland with almost no trees.

prairie a large, open grassland with very few trees

habitat the place where a plant or animal usually lives

Vocabulary in Context

Look for clues to the meanings of unfamiliar words within or beyond the sentence the word appears in. Find the word *bison*. <u>Underline</u> the synonym, or the word that means the same as *bison*.

American bison

7 Many different kinds of grasses grow on the prairie. There are tallgrass, mixed-grass, and short-grass prairies.

8 **Bluestem** and Indian grass are the tallest grasses on the prairie.

9 **American bison** roam the prairies. Another name for bison is buffalo.

10   Bison and deer are prairie **grazers**, which means they feed on prairie grasses.

Deer graze on grass, leaves, bark, and acorns.

CLOSE READ

Text Features

Underline the label that helps you locate the burrow in the photo.

Confirm Predictions

Did the facts in the text match the prediction you made before reading? What information in the text surprised you?

burrows holes or tunnels in the ground that are made by a small animal

burrow

11 Many prairie animals live in underground holes called **burrows**. Badgers, black-footed ferrets, prairie dogs, and burrowing owls all spend time in these holes.

Most owls live in trees. But burrowing owls live in underground holes!

Text Features

Underline the part of the photo caption that tells you where prairie dogs got their name.

colonies groups of animals that live in one place

12   Prairie dog burrows connect to form groups, or **colonies**. These colonies are almost like underground towns.

Prairie dogs got their name from the loud barking noise they make.

13 The prairie is an exciting place to explore! Peek among the tall grasses. You'll meet this black-footed ferret and other truly amazing animals that live in this habitat!

Text Features

Underline the heading that tells you the main topic of these two pages.

Confirm or Adjust Predictions

Did you need to adjust or revise your prediction based on information in the text?

A Day in the Life of a Rattlesnake

How does a rattlesnake spend most of its time?

14   A rattlesnake hides in burrows or under rocks or plants.

What does a rattlesnake eat?

15   A rattlesnake eats mice, ground squirrels, and younger prairie dogs and rabbits.

274

What are a rattlesnake's enemies?

16 Humans, hawks, and eagles are a rattlesnake's enemies.

Does a rattlesnake have a special trick?

17 A rattlesnake rattles its tail as a warning to stay away.

Your New Words

1 **American bison** (uh-**mer**-uh-kuhn **bye**-suhn) prairie animals with large heads and high, humped shoulders

2 **bluestem** (**blu**-stehm) one of the tallest types of prairie grass

3 **burrows** (**bur**-ohz) holes or tunnels in the ground that are made by a small animal

4 **colonies** (**kol**-uh-neez) groups of animals that live in one place

5 **grazers** (**grayz**-urz) animals that feed on growing grasses

6 **habitat** (**hab**-uh-tat) the place where a plant or animal usually lives

7 **prairie** (**prer**-ee) a large, open grassland with very few trees

Index

CLOSE READ

Text Features

Underline the page number where you can learn more about deer.

Develop Vocabulary

MY TURN Use the glossary that follows the text to determine the meaning of each word below. Write each word's meaning.

Word	Meaning
prairie	a large, open grassland with very few trees
habitat	
grazers	
burrows	
colonies	

Check for Understanding

MY TURN Write brief comments to answer the questions. Look back at the text.

1. What makes this text an informational text?

_____

_____

----

2. Why did the author include a glossary?

_____

_____

_____

----

3. How are prairie dogs and burrowing owls alike? Include text evidence.

_____

_____

Use Text Features and Graphics

Authors choose text features and graphics to help readers locate, or find, information.

- **Headings** tell the topics of the text.
- **Photos** show what the text describes.
- **Captions** tell what a picture shows.
- **Bold words** are words to learn and remember.

MY TURN Go to the Close Read notes. Underline text features. Use features and graphics to locate information to complete the chart.

Text Feature Author Used	Information I Found
label on a photo	It helped me find the burrow in the photo.

Make and Confirm Predictions

Use headings, labels, captions, and other text features to predict what a text will be about. As you read, confirm or correct your prediction.

MY TURN Go back to the Close Read note on the second page of the text. Follow the directions to highlight the text. Use your predictions and the evidence you highlighted to complete the chart.

Text Features	I predicted...	Now I know...
Title		
Photos		
Bold words		

Reflect and Share

Write to Sources

Think about everything you learned about prairies this week. Write a paragraph explaining how plants and animals work together on a prairie to help each other survive.

Use Facts to Develop a Main Idea

When you write an informational paragraph, be sure to use facts. The facts should relate to the main idea of your paragraph.

- Decide on the main idea of your paragraph.
- Find facts in the texts you read that support your main idea.

Write a sentence that tells your main idea. In your own words, write facts that help develop your main idea.

Weekly Question

What patterns can we see on a prairie?

I can use language to make connections between reading and writing informational text.

Academic Vocabulary

Synonyms are words that mean the same or almost the same thing. You can find synonyms in a book or online source called a thesaurus.

MY TURN Use a thesaurus. Write a synonym for each of the words.

Word	Synonym
behave	act
proof	
identification	
different	

Read Like a Writer, Write for a Reader

Authors choose words for specific purposes. An author uses descriptions to help you create mental images of people, places, and things to make a text come alive.

Description	What I Picture in My Mind
"A rattlesnake shakes its tail to warn its enemies."	I picture the snake moving its tail back and forth very quickly.

TURN and TALK Discuss the descriptive words in this sentence: **You watch a prairie dog dive into a hole.** How does the author help you picture prairie dogs?

Rewrite this sentence using more descriptive words: **Deer eat grass and other things.**

_____

- - - - - - - - - - - - - - - - -

_____

_____

- - - - - - - - - - - - - - - - -

_____

Spell Words with Long a: ai, ay, ea

Long **a** can be spelled **ai**, **ay**, and **ea**.

MY TURN Sort and spell the Spelling Words by their long **a** vowel pattern. Then write the My Words to Know.

ai

brain

_____

_____

ay

_____

_____

_____

_____

_____

_____

ea

_____

_____

_____

My Words to Know

_____

_____

_____

Spelling Words

pay
break
brain
great
paint
Sunday
Monday
Thursday
Friday
Saturday

My Words to Know

air
change

Irregular Plural Nouns

Irregular plural nouns do not follow a spelling rule to become plural. Look at these examples.

Singular Noun	Plural Noun
child	children
fish	fish
foot	feet
mouse	mice
tooth	teeth

MY TURN Edit this draft by crossing out the incorrect plural nouns and writing the correct word above. The first one is done for you.

children

The ~~childs~~ in my classroom are writing a story together. It

is about a family of mouses. The story is funny. It tells how

each mouse likes to use its foots to play games and likes to

use its tooth to hold a fishing pole and catch fishes.

I can use elements of informational text to write a list article.

Topic and Main Idea

An author chooses a **topic** to write about. The **main**, or **central, idea** is the most important information about that topic.

MY TURN Fill in the chart below using informational texts from your classroom library.

Title	Topic	Main Idea

Develop Details

An author uses information to support the main, or central, idea. Examples might include specific and relevant details, facts, and definitions.

Main Idea
There are many patterns in nature.

Specific and relevant details are small pieces of information.

Many different animals have patterns on their fur, feathers, or skin.

Facts give information that can be proved to be true.

A snake's species can be determined by the pattern on its skin.

Definitions tell the meanings of words or ideas.

A pattern is a design that is repeated over and over.

MY TURN In your writer's notebook, plan the details for your list article. Use your plan to develop a draft.

Graphic Features

MY TURN Read "The Oak Tree." Draw two graphic features that illustrate, or show, what the text is saying. <u>Underline</u> the sentences that your graphic features tell about.

The Oak Tree

A tall oak tree grows from one small round acorn. The tree stands next to the lake across from our school. Its green leaves reach up to the sky.

In the fall, the leaves change. They turn many colors and then fall.

The big tree stays in the winter without leaves. In spring, green leaves grow back.

Graphic Feature 1	Graphic Feature 2

Circle of Seasons

1 In winter, snowflakes softly fall,
Like leaves of white upon us all.

4 In autumn, dry leaves drop, and then
The season circle starts again!

2 In spring, small seeds begin to bud. Green stems appear across the mud.

How does a tree show patterns as seasons change?

TURN and TALK

Read the poem. Look at the pictures and discuss what you know about seasons. How does the tree in the pictures change from season to season?

3 In summer, sunflowers grow so high, Their yellow petals touch the sky.

Recognize Changes in Words

SEE and SAY You can recognize new words made by changing the middle sound, or phoneme, in a word. Say the name of the pictures.

What middle sound changed from the first picture to the second?

What middle sound changed from the second picture to the third?

MY TURN Work with a partner. Name the pictures. Say what sound changed in the second picture.

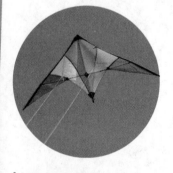 

Vowel Digraph ie

The vowel team, or digraph, **ie** can stand for the long **i** sound or the long **e** sound.

MY TURN Read each word below and listen for the long **i** or long **e** sound.

Long i	Long e
t<u>ie</u>	p<u>ie</u>ce
p<u>ie</u>	th<u>ie</u>f
l<u>ie</u>	f<u>ie</u>ld
tr<u>ie</u>d	bel<u>ie</u>ve

TURN and TALK Read these sentences with a partner. Underline the words that have the long **i** sound or the long **e** sound spelled **ie**.

1. Maya cried when she dropped her piece of fruit pie.

2. Jan tried to write a brief story about a chief with a tie.

Vowel Digraph ie

MY TURN Read the words in the box. Then write a word from the box to name each picture.

piece	field	tie	pie	shield	chief

piece

_____

_____

_____

_____

_____

MY TURN Write a sentence about one of the pictures above using the word that names it.

_____

_____

My Words to Know

MY TURN Read the words in the box. Then identify and underline the words in the sentences. One is done for you.

animal	point	study

1. Our teacher told us to **point** to the answer.

2. "That animal is a fox," said Kim.

3. Don't forget to study for the test!

4. Point to the picture you like best.

Now write your own sentence for each word.

_____

_____

_____

_____

TURN and TALK Work with a partner. Read and discuss each other's sentences.

My Learning Goal

I can learn more about patterns in nature by reading a story about how a tree affects a boy's life.

Realistic Fiction

Realistic fiction is a made-up story that could happen in real life. It has:

- a **plot,** or set of **events,** that is believable. It often has a conflict and a resolution, or a solution to the problem

- **characters** that are like people you might know

- a **setting** that could be real

Establish Purpose The purpose for reading assigned and self-selected realistic fiction is often to enjoy a good story that has a plot and a setting that could be true.

TURNand**TALK** Tell your partner your purpose or purposes for reading *The Seasons of Arnold's Apple Tree.* For example, you may want to find out who Arnold is and what the seasons are that the title mentions.

Realistic Fiction Anchor Chart

Realistic fiction is a made-up story that could happen in real life.

Realistic fiction has

a setting that could be like a place you know

a plot that could be true

characters who might be like people you know

a beginning, middle, and end

The Seasons of Arnold's Apple Tree

Preview Vocabulary

Look for these words as you read *The Seasons of Arnold's Apple Tree.*

carefully	quietly	rustle	glow	decorates

First Read

Read for the purpose you set.

Look at illustrations to help you understand the text.

Ask questions about the sequence of events.

Talk about what you found most interesting.

Meet the Author

Gail Gibbons made picture books as a child. After college, she did artwork for television shows. Then she wrote a book for children. Now, she writes and illustrates mostly nonfiction children's books. She has written over 170 books!

Genre Realistic Fiction

The Seasons of Arnold's Apple Tree

by Gail Gibbons

AUDIO

Audio with Highlighting

ANNOTATE

Understand Setting and Plot

Underline the words that describe the setting where Arnold is. Then underline the words that tell why Arnold is there.

1 **A**rnold climbs up high into the branches of the apple tree.

2 He can see far, far away in every direction.

3 This is Arnold's very own secret place.
   This is Arnold's apple tree.

4 Arnold's tree keeps him very busy all
   through the year.

Understand Setting and Plot

<u>Underline</u> the text that describes what Arnold sees happening to his tree in spring. Think about how the picture helps you understand this event.

5   **I**t is spring.

6   Arnold watches the small buds grow on his apple tree.

7   Some of the buds develop into sweet-smelling apple blossoms.

8 Carefully and quietly, Arnold watches bees collect nectar from the blossoms to make honey.

HONEYBEE AND APPLE BLOSSOMS
The honeybee makes honey from nectar, the sweet juice found in flowers.

303

Understand Setting and Plot

<u>Underline</u> the word that names what Arnold builds for his tree. Think about how the first picture helps you understand one step Arnold takes to build it.

9 Arnold makes a swing for his apple tree.

10 He weaves an apple-blossom wreath
and hangs it from a branch.

Visualize Details

Highlight details that can help you form a picture in your mind of the branches that Arnold brings to his family.

11   Arnold picks an armful of apple blossoms and brings it to his family.

12 They make a flower arrangement together.

Understand Setting and Plot

<u>Underline</u> the text that describes what happens to Arnold's tree in summer. Think about how the picture helps you understand this event.

rustle make a soft sound of two things rubbing together

13 **I**t is summer.

14 Arnold's apple tree has big, green leaves that rustle in the wind.

15 Arnold builds a tree house.

CLOSE READ

Visualize Details

Highlight words that can help you form a picture in your mind of how the apple tree helps Arnold in summer.

16 His apple tree shades him from the hot summer sun.

17   The green leaves shelter him during a summer shower.

18 Arnold watches small apples begin to
grow from where the blossoms used to
be. They grow bigger, bigger . . .

19 and bigger.

20 With some of the big, green apples, Arnold does a juggling act for his tree friend.

CLOSE READ

Vocabulary in Context

Sometimes you can figure out the meaning of a word by using words nearby and the picture. Underline words near **juggling** that help you understand what **juggling** means.

Understand Setting and Plot

Underline the text that tells how the tree's leaves change in fall. How is this picture different from the picture of Arnold's tree in spring?

21   **I**t is fall.

22   Arnold's apple tree now has big, red, tasty apples.

23   The green leaves have turned golden. They drift to the ground.

24   Arnold gathers some of the leaves and brings them up to his tree house to make a soft floor to lie on.

25   Arnold shakes the branches and red apples fall to the ground.

26   He puts them in a basket and takes them home.

27 Arnold and his family make apple pies
with apples from Arnold's apple tree.

28 They put the rest of the apples into a
cider press and make fresh apple cider.

29 On Halloween Day, Arnold decorates some of the biggest apples.

30 They glow in the moonlight under his tree on Halloween night.

CLOSE READ

Visualize Details

Highlight words that can help you picture the apples on Halloween night.

decorates makes something look pretty by putting something on it

glow to shine, or put out light

Understand Setting and Plot

Underline the words that describe what happens to the tree branches in winter. Think about how the picture helps you understand this event.

31 It is winter.

32 Snow falls. It is quiet. The branches of Arnold's apple tree are bare.

33 Arnold hangs strings of popcorn and berries on them for the winter birds to eat.

34 He builds a snow fort around the bottom of his tree.

35   Arnold builds a snowman to keep him
and his tree company during the winter.

36 The snow melts away.

37 It is spring again. . . .

Visualize Details

Highlight words that can help you picture what happens in spring.

Develop Vocabulary

Words that end in **-ly** often tell how something is done.

MY TURN Underline the boxed words that end in **-ly**, and complete items 1–3. For items 4–6, write the word that goes with each word group.

carefully	quietly	rustle	glow	decorates

1. Slowly means done in a slow way.

2. Done in a careful way is done _____

3. Quietly means _____

4. candle, fireplace, firefly, _____

5. leaves in wind, moving papers, _____

6. ties a ribbon on a gift, hangs balloons in the room, _____

Check for Understanding

MY TURN Write the answers to the questions. Look back at the text to answer the questions.

1. Could this story happen in real life? Why or why not?

_____

_____

_____

_____

2. How does the author organize the events in the story? Why?

_____

_____

_____

_____

_____

3. The story ends with the words "It is spring again. . . ." What do you think will happen next?

_____

_____

_____

_____

Understand Setting and Plot

Describing a story's **setting** can help you see its importance. Where and when a story happens affects **plot elements**, including the main events, the conflict, and the story's resolution.

MY TURN Partner read the text aloud. Go to the Close Read notes. Use the parts you underlined together with other text evidence and illustrations to complete the chart.

Paragraphs	Describe Setting: Where and When?	Describe Plot Elements: What Happens?
5, 6	spring; an apple tree with small buds	Arnold watches the small buds grow.
13–15		
21–26		
31–33		

Visualize Details

When you visualize details as you read, you picture in your mind what the author is describing. Visualizing makes the story come alive and helps you understand the setting and plot.

MY TURN Go back to the Close Read notes labeled Visualize Details. Follow the directions to highlight words. Choose a detail that you highlighted. Close your eyes and create your own mental image to deepen your understanding. Then draw what you visualized. Explain your picture to a partner.

The detail I visualized is _____.

Reflect and Share

Talk About It

Think about this story and other stories you have read that take place in the country. How does spending time in nature affect how the characters act and how they feel? Why is the setting important in these stories?

Make Comments That Support Your Ideas

As you talk about texts you have read, it is important to give text evidence that supports your ideas.

- State your ideas clearly.

- Use details from the text that support your points.

- Answer the question using multi-word responses, or answers of more than one word.

Use these sentence starters to help you make relevant comments.

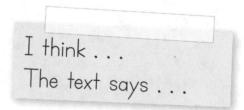

I think . . .
The text says . . .

Weekly Question

How does a tree show patterns as seasons change?

I can use language to make connections between reading and writing informational text.

My Learning Goal

Academic Vocabulary

Context clues within and beyond a sentence can help you determine the meanings of unfamiliar words.

MY TURN Circle the context clues that help you understand each **bold** word or phrase. Then write a meaning for the word or phrase.

1. Melly wore two different colored socks today. When I saw her smile, I knew it was no accident. She wore those socks **by design**.

   by design: _____.

2. Horses and zebras have some **similarities**. They both have four legs, hooves, a long face, a mane, and a tail.

   similarities: _____.

Read Like a Writer, Write for a Reader

Authors use both short sentences and long sentences to make their writing interesting.

Author's Writing	How the Sentences Vary
"Snow falls. It is quiet. The branches of Arnold's apple tree are bare. Arnold hangs strings of popcorn and berries on them for the winter birds to eat."	The first two sentences are short. The last two sentences are long. It sounds interesting to read them all together.

MY TURN Write four sentences that describe a night. Write two short and two long sentences.

S t

Spell Words with ie

The vowel team **ie** spells the long **e** or the long **i** sound.

MY TURN Sort and spell the Spelling Words by their vowel pattern. Then write the My Words to Know.

Write the words with **ie** that have the long **e** sound.

chief

_____   _____

_____   _____

_____   _____

_____   _____

_____   _____

Write the words with **ie** that have the long **i** sound.

_____   _____

_____   _____

My Words to Know

_____   _____

_____   _____

Spelling Words

chief

field

pie

thief

tie

niece

brief

piece

believe

goalie

My Words to Know

animal

study

Common and Proper Nouns

A **common noun** names any person, place, or thing. A **proper noun** names a particular person, place, or thing. Proper nouns begin with capital letters.

Common Nouns: boy, teacher, city, month, holiday

Proper Nouns: Lin, Ms. Garza, Austin, May, Labor Day

MY TURN Edit this draft. Make sure proper nouns begin with capital letters and common nouns do not. Cross out each incorrect letter and write the correct letter above it. The first one is done for you.

b
My ~~B~~irthday is in february. I can celebrate

at School because it's winter. My friend

ann's birthday is in july. Our Teacher, mr. kim,

said the class will go to rockwood park on

the last day of school. On that day, we'll

celebrate everyone's Summer birthdays!

Did you remember to capitalize the months?

I can use elements of informational text to write a list article.

My Learning Goal

Introduction and Conclusion

An author writes an **introduction** and a **conclusion** to a list article. The introduction tells the main, or central, idea. The conclusion summarizes it.

Introduction

What kinds of ideas are in your list article? What is the most important idea?

Conclusion

What important ideas from your article can you summarize, or tell briefly?

MY TURN Plan the introduction and conclusion for your list article. Write them in your writer's notebook.

Organize Details

An author organizes details. One way to organize is to put the most important information first.

Item in List	Details
1. Mammals	Have fur or hair Feed their babies with milk
2. Birds	Have feathers Feathers keep them warm
3. Reptiles	Have scales Scales help protect their bodies

MY TURN Write three items for your list article. Organize the details for each item to develop your draft.

Item in List	Details

Text Features

Authors use text features when they write a list article. Examples of text features are titles and bold type. The **title** identifies the topic. The **title** tells what the text will be about.

Bold type tells the reader to pay special attention. Things in **bold type** are important.

MY TURN Develop the structure of your list article. Decide how you will use text features to organize your draft. Write your ideas.

The title of my list article will be:

_____

_____

_____

These are things I will put in bold type:

_____

_____

_____

_____

ANIMALS
and Their Young

Young elephants travel with their mothers in herds. They are protected by the herd.

A baby gorilla does not leave its mother for the first five months. The father stays nearby and protects them both.

Clownfish parents clean a place to lay eggs. Then they wave their fins to move water over their eggs. Air in moving water helps the baby fish develop.

Father and mother flamingoes take turns sitting on their nest to keep the egg warm. When the baby hatches, both parents feed it with a food they make in their own bodies. The food turns the baby pink!

Weekly Question

How do patterns of behavior in animals help keep their young safe?

TURN and TALK

Look at the pictures and read the text about animals and their young. How do animal parents help their babies? Underline the ways.

Talk about it with a partner.

Manipulate Sounds

SEE *and* **SAY** Say the name of the picture. What sound do you hear at the beginning? What sound do you hear at the end? When you manipulate sounds, you switch sounds to get a new word. If you manipulate, or switch, the beginning and ending sounds in **bat**, you get the new word **tab**.

Say the name of the first picture. What sound do you hear at the beginning? What sound do you hear at the end? Switch the sounds in the word. What is the new word? Repeat for the other two pictures.

TURN *and* **TALK** Work with a partner. Manipulate, or change, the sounds in the words **mane**, **bus**, and **cub**.

Long e: ee, ea, ey, y

You can hear the long **e** sound in words with **ee**, **ea**, **ey**, and **y**. You will often see **ey** and **y** at the end of words.

MY TURN Read, or decode, the words below. Listen for the long **e** sound.

ee	ea	ey	y
feel	leap	key	very
sleep	dream	money	baby
teeth	teach	donkey	happy

TURN and TALK Reread the words in the chart with a partner. Underline the letters that make the long **e** sound in each word. Then take turns using the words in sentences. Use one word from each spelling pattern.

Long e: ee, ea, ey, y

MY TURN <u>Underline</u> the letters that make the long **e** sound in each word. Then write a sentence that uses each word. Read your sentences.

1. feet My feet are big.

2. donkey

3. many

4. keep

5. beak

6. street

7. leash

My Words to Know

MY TURN Read the words in the box. Identify and <u>underline</u> them in the sentences. One is done for you.

letter	answer	page

1. Please turn to <u>page</u> 20 in your books.

2. I got a letter from my grandpa.

3. Turn the page to read the rest of the story.

4. Did you answer yes or no?

MY TURN Write the word that goes with each clue.

_____

5. It comes in the mail. _____

_____

6. It is something you turn. _____

_____

7. It follows a question. _____

TURN and TALK Work with a partner. One partner gives a clue and the other partner guesses the word.

My Learning Goal I can learn about patterns in nature by reading a story about penguins.

Fiction

Fiction is a story that did not really happen. Authors make up the events, setting, and characters when they write fiction. In fiction:

- **animal characters** often talk and act like people.

- authors give characters **traits** by telling how they look, act, think, and feel.

- characters can change because of the events that happen.

Think of what you already know about people to understand characters better.

TURN and TALK Discuss with a partner how fiction and informational texts are different from each other.

Fiction Anchor Chart

Purpose

To entertain or tell a story about characters

Character Traits

External

tall

walks slowly

usually speaks softly

Internal

kind

smart

usually feels calm

What's in the Egg, Little Pip?

Preview Vocabulary

Look for these words as you read *What's in the Egg, Little Pip?*

oval	waddle	huddled	penguin	flock

First Read

Read to understand the author's message.

Look at illustrations to help you understand the text.

Ask what this text is about.

Talk about the author's message about life.

Meet the Author

Karma Wilson has always loved reading. She began writing books for children when she had children of her own. She lives with her family, two dogs, a cat, and four horses on a ranch in Montana.

What's in the Egg, Little Pip?

by **Karma Wilson**
illustrated by **Jane Chapman**

 AUDIO

Audio with Highlighting

 ANNOTATE

Make Inferences

Sometimes the author gives you a clue to how someone feels. Highlight the words that are a clue to why Pip might not like the Egg.

oval having the shape of an egg

1   Little Pip stared at the Egg. The large, white oval rested on Mama's feet just under her soft, warm belly. Pip used to sleep there, but there was no room for her now, not since the Egg. Mama and Papa asked, "What do you think, Little Pip?"

2   Pip shrugged. She wasn't sure.

3 Mama and Papa had talked about the Egg for a long time. Yesterday morning they had woken Pip and said, "The Egg is finally here, Little Pip!" As they showed her the Egg they sang this song:

4 *"The Egg, the Egg, the lovely Egg,*
a wonderful, glorious sight.
A sister or brother for sweet Little Pip
will soon make our family just right."

Describe and Understand Characters

Underline a word that describes the look on Pip's face.

5   Pip frowned. The Egg didn't look like much.

6   "Our family is just right," Pip said. "That old Egg can't make it better."

7   Mama nuzzled Pip and said, "Just wait. You may be surprised. And now, Papa, it's time for you to take over."

8 Mama carefully nudged the Egg and tucked it on Papa's feet. Then Papa nestled down onto the Egg.

9 "Where are you going, Mama?" Pip asked.

10 "I need to go fish to bring food for you," Mama said, "but somebody must always be with the Egg to keep it warm. So Papa will watch the Egg while I fish, and I will watch the Egg when Papa fishes."

11　"Can I go with you?" Pip pleaded.

12　Mama smiled and shook her head. "You stay and help Papa keep the Egg warm and safe. We must be ready for any storms. We don't want the Egg to get cold. We'll need you."

13 Pip sighed. "I'm too little to help. I'm still your baby."

14 Mama shook her head. "You have grown up so much, Little Pip. You're big enough to help Papa. You're big enough to help me. You're even big enough to help the Egg! Remember that. But don't worry; you will always be our baby."

Make Inferences

Highlight the text that helps you understand, or make an inference, that Pip is still important to her parents.

Describe and Understand Characters

Underline the part of the text that shows how Pip feels when Mama leaves.

waddle to walk with short steps while swinging the body from side to side

15 Pip wasn't so sure. As she watched her mama waddle away, a tear slipped down her cheek. Now it was just her and Papa . . . oh, and the Egg.

16 Later that day Pip chirped, "Papa, let's slide on the ice."

17 Papa shook his head. "I can't leave the Egg, Little Pip."

18 Pip frowned. "Not even for a minute?"

19 "Not even for a second."

20 "But isn't it boring?"

21 "A little," said Papa.

22 "Then why do you do it?" Pip asked.

23 Papa smiled. "That's what families do, Little Pip. I did the same for you when you were just an egg."

24 Pip couldn't imagine that she was ever just an egg. Why had Mama and Papa even wanted the Egg? *I should be enough!* thought Pip.

25 She wandered off to think, and as she slumped along she sang,

26   *"The Egg, the Egg, it's all the Egg.*
Nobody cares about me.
I liked it best before the Egg,
back when our family was three."

27   Little Pip felt so all alone that she decided to look for her best friend, Merry. "You want to go slide?" she asked.

28   "I guess," said Merry. She didn't seem her usual cheerful self.

Describe and Understand Characters

Underline the text that tells what Pip does to help herself feel better.

Describe and Understand Characters

<u>Underline</u> the text that tells what Merry does that shows how she feels about her family's Egg.

29 "Does your family have an egg too?" asked Pip.

30 Merry nodded and stamped her foot. "I don't see the fuss about the Egg. It just sits there and does nothing."

31 "I know," said Pip. "But it's all Mama and Papa ever talk about or think about anymore. I want to forget about the Eggs. Let's slide!"

32 And so they did.

WHOOP!

WHEEE!

WHISH!

33 They didn't think about the Eggs again.

34 But suddenly the sun disappeared behind a thick, black cloud.

35 **"A storm!"** squealed Pip.

36 "We must run! **Hurry!"**

37 "We're too little," said Merry. "We can't!"

38 Pip ruffled her feathers and puffed out her chest.

39 "My mama said I'm big enough to help the Egg. So are you. We have to go help. Now **RUN!**"

40 They raced the cloud all the way home.

Vocabulary In Context

You can use context within a sentence and beyond it to determine the meaning of a phrase. Underline words that help you understand the meaning of **puffed out**.

CLOSE READ

Make Inferences

Highlight the text that helps you understand that Papa and Pip care about the Egg.

huddled crowded together

41 Just as they reached camp, frozen sleet started to fall in cold, stinging drops. Pip snuggled tight against her papa, helping to shield the Egg.

42 There they huddled, and there they waited.

43 And waited.

44 And waited.

CLOSE READ

Make Inferences

Highlight the text that helps you understand that Pip is hungry.

45 Finally Mama returned. Pip's tummy growled.

46 She was glad to eat the fish Mama had brought back for them.

47 But then Papa had to go fishing.

48 Storms came and went, and the Egg always had to be kept warm. Pip, Mama, and Papa huddled around the Egg for many weeks. Sometimes Mama left to fish, sometimes Papa, but Pip always stayed with the Egg.

49 Then one bright, sunny day, while Mama was away fishing . . .

50 **CHIP,**
CHIP,
CRACK.

51 "The Egg is broken, Papa!" Pip cried, and buried her head into Papa's chest. All that work, for nothing.

Craaaaaaack.

52 Pip gasped. The Egg was gone.

53 In its place sat a beautiful penguin chick.

54 "It's a chick! A chick, Papa!"

55 "Little Pip, meet your brother."

CLOSE READ

Describe and Understand Characters

<u>Underline</u> what Pip says that shows she is excited now that the Egg has hatched.

penguin a short-legged, black-and-white seabird that cannot fly and that lives in or near the Antarctic

flock a group of
animals such as
birds

56 At the beach lots of penguins were
squawking and talking. Pip saw a
flock of penguins just back from
fishing. Mama! She was home.

57 Mama sighed with happiness. "He
looks just like you when you were a
baby, Pip!"

58 Pip smiled. "I was that small?"

59 "Oh yes," said Mama. "Just that
small."

60 Pip looked at her new brother and she sang,

"Welcome, chick, you lovely chick.
What a wonderful, glorious sight.
Little brother, I name you Sam.
You make our family just right."

61 Little Pip looked around and saw all the penguin families snuggling new chicks in their pebbly nests. Pip waved to Merry and Merry waved back, a huge smile on her face.

62 Pip smiled too.

63 Everything felt just right.

Make Inferences

<u>Underline</u> details that show that Pip's feelings about having a new family member have changed.

Develop Vocabulary

MY TURN Related words can have almost the same meanings. Look at the words in the second column. Write the word whose meaning is closest to the meaning of the word in the first column.

Word	Related Words	Word Closest in Meaning
oval	shape circle	circle
waddle	walk jog	
huddled	crowded together	
flock	pair group	

MY TURN Which word below best describes **penguin** parents?

kind	caring	worried

Check for Understanding

MY TURN Write brief comments to answer the questions. Look back at the text.

1. What makes this text fiction?

_____

- -

_____

- -

_____

2. How does the dialogue help you understand the story?

_____

- -

_____

- -

_____

3. How will Pip probably feel if Mama lays another egg next year? Use text evidence to explain your answer.

_____

- -

_____

- -

_____

Describe and Understand Characters

Authors often describe the main characters' **external traits,** or how they look and what they do and say. You can figure out the main characters' **internal traits,** or what they think or feel, from their words and actions.

MY TURN Go to the Close Read notes. Underline words that describe a character's traits. Use the parts you underlined about Pip to complete the chart.

Event	Pip's Actions	Describe How Pip Feels
Mama and Papa sing a happy song about the Egg.	Pip frowns.	She thinks the family is fine without the Egg.
Mama leaves to find food.		
Papa has to stay with the Egg.		
The Egg hatches and Pip meets her brother.		

Make Inferences

To make an inference, you combine what you already know with evidence in a story. Then you decide what the author wants you to understand. A story often has a conflict that gets resolved. Use what the characters say and do to make inferences about the conflict.

👀 MY TURN Go back to the Close Read notes. Read the text aloud with a partner. Highlight the words that help you make inferences. Then complete the chart.

Paragraphs	What I Already Know	My Inferences
1	A new baby can make older children feel less important.	What is the conflict?
41		
60–63		What is the resolution?

Reflect and Share

Write to Sources

This week you read about animals that keep their young safe. Why is it important for animals to protect their babies? Write your response in a paragraph on a separate sheet of paper.

Organize Your Writing

Before you write a paragraph, decide how to organize it.

- Think of a topic sentence that tells what your paragraph will be about.
- Find at least two examples that support your idea.
- Think of a closing sentence that tells your main point.

In your paragraph, describe each of your examples. Use details from the texts you read this week. Tell why your examples are important.

Weekly Question

How do patterns of behavior in animals help keep their young safe?

I can use language to make connections between reading and writing.

My Learning Goal

Academic Vocabulary

Word parts can help you figure out the meanings of words. Sometimes a word is made up of a base word and an ending.

design + -er = designer

MY TURN Add the ending **-er** or **-or** to each base word to build a new word.

design + -er = *designer*

teach + -er = _____

visit + -or = _____

act + -or = _____

What do you think the endings **-er** and **-or** mean?

_____

Read Like a Writer, Write for a Reader

Dialogue is the words that characters say to each other. Each character has a voice, or way of speaking. Authors use dialogue to help readers know how the characters feel and what they are like.

What the Character Says	What It Shows About the Character
"Our family is just right," Pip said. "That old Egg can't make it better."	Pip sounds angry. She is also not afraid to say what she is feeling.
"But don't worry; you will always be our baby."	Mama says loving things to make Pip feel better.

MY TURN Write a dialogue between two animals that shows what each character is like.

_____

_____

_____

Spell Words with Long e: ee, ea, ey, y

Long **e** can be spelled with **ee**, **ea**, **ey**, or **y**.

MY TURN Sort the Spelling Words by how they are spelled. Then write the My Words to Know.

ee

street

ea

ey

My Words to Know

y

Spelling Words

each
team
street
key
read
feel
deep
party
easy
beach

My Words to Know

letter
answer

Possessive Nouns

A noun can show who owns something. Add **'s** to a singular noun. Add **'** to a plural noun that ends in **s**.

Belongs to one	Belongs to more than one
one bear's den	four bears' dens
one farmer's land	many farmers' lands

MY TURN Edit this draft. Cross out each incorrect possessive noun. Write the correct possessive noun above it. The first one is done for you.

On my Aunt ~~Joans'~~ Joan's day off, we went to the park. Many

tree's leaves were turning red and yellow. We saw flocks

of birds flying. Some bird's feathers were bright blue.

A mans' dogs wagged their tails when they saw us.

I can use elements of informational text to write a list article.

My Learning Goal

Complete Sentences with Subject-Verb Agreement

Authors edit their writing to make sure they have used complete sentences. A complete sentence has a subject and a predicate. Authors also check that the subject and verb in each sentence agree. Here are examples of an author's edits:

eat   are   Penguins c
Penguins ~~eats~~ fish. They ~~is~~ birds. ^Cannot fly.

MY TURN Edit the draft. Cross out each verb that does not agree with the subject. Write the correct verb above. Then edit your list article for complete sentences and for subject-verb agreement.

A penguin swim fast. Its flippers acts like paddles. Its

webbed feet helps too. Sometimes a penguin leap up out

of the water. Then dives back in.

375

Nouns

Authors edit their writing to make sure they have used nouns correctly.

- A common noun names any person, animal, place, or thing: **girl**.

- A proper noun begins with a capital letter and names a particular person, animal, place, or thing: **Alia**.

- A singular noun names one: **boy**.

- A plural noun names more than one: **boys**.

Here is an example of an author's edit:

> Penguin mothers lay ~~egges~~ eggs in the ~~S~~pring. s

MY TURN Edit the draft. Cross out incorrect letters or nouns and write the correct letters or nouns above. Then edit your list article. Make sure you have used nouns correctly.

> Ms. warren told us that male penguins keep the eggs warm. They roll them onto their feets and cover them up. Then the Fathers stand together to stay warm.

Prepositions and Prepositional Phrases

Authors edit their writing to make sure they have used prepositions and prepositional phrases correctly.

- A **preposition** is a word such as **with, in, for,** or **by.**
- A preposition is the first word in a group of words called a **prepositional phrase:**

  The dog is **in the house.**

Here is an example of an author's edit:

> The egg rests ~~over~~ under the mother penguin's belly.

MY TURN Edit the draft. Cross out each incorrect preposition. Write the correct preposition above it. Then edit your list article. Make sure you have used prepositions and prepositional phrases correctly.

> The penguins slide in the ice. They dive onto the water.
> They swim by the surface. Then they leap over it to take a
> breath of air.

ANIMALS
on the Move

Some animals migrate. They move from one place to another at certain times of the year. Animal migrations happen all over the world.

Hundreds of **pronghorns** migrate in western North America. The animals travel 150 miles to graze in their winter feeding grounds.

North America

Gray whales spend the winter in warmer ocean waters. When the season changes, the whales migrate to spend the summer in cooler climates.

South America

Weekly Question

What migration patterns do we see in some animals?

Millions of **wildebeests** migrate across a great plain in Africa every year. Wildebeests travel great distances to find water in the dry season.

Africa

 **MY TURN** Look at the pictures and read the captions. <u>Underline</u> the different reasons the animals migrate. How does migration help animals? What other animals do you know that migrate?

Manipulate Sounds

SEE and SAY When you manipulate, or change, the sounds in a word, you make a new word. Say the beginning and ending sounds of the name for the picture. Now switch the beginning sound and the ending sound to make a new word.

Change, or manipulate, the beginning and ending sounds you hear in these picture names to make a new word.

TURN and TALK Work with a partner. Manipulate, or change, the sounds in the words **step**, **net**, and **pat**.

Long o: o, oa, ow

Long **o** can be spelled **o**, **oa**, and **ow**. **Oa** and **ow** are vowel teams, or digraphs.

oval

g**oa**t

cr**ow**

MY TURN Read, or decode, each word and listen for the long **o** sound. See how long **o** is spelled.

o	oa	ow
cold	boat	grow
open	toast	pillow
only	throat	below

TURN and TALK Read the sentences with a partner. Underline the spellings for long **o**.

1. The gold boat floated slowly on the ocean.

2. The crow flew over the oak tree.

Long o: o, oa, ow

MY TURN Read the words in the box. Write words from the box to complete the sentences.

toad	follow	cold	most
croaked	blows	show	toast

1. When the wind blows , it is _____ .

2. If you _____ me the way, I'll _____ you.

3. The big _____ hopped under the leaf and _____ _____.

4. Luke ate _____ of the _____ but left a piece for me.

My Words to Know

MY TURN Read the words in the box. Then read the sentences. Identify and underline the words in the sentences.

near	food	try

We have <u>food</u> for the picnic. The water is near the plates. Try not to spill it. The food is yummy!

MY TURN Write the word that rhymes with each word.

rude _____

here _____

tie _____

> The vowel sounds in the rhyming words are the same but are spelled differently.

TURN and TALK Work with a partner. Make up a sentence with one of the words. Say "blank" instead of the word. Have your partner guess the word. Take turns.

My Learning Goal I can read informational text and use its features to understand more about a topic.

Spotlight on Genre

Informational Text

Informational text tells about real people, animals, places, or events. **Text features** and **graphics** can help you locate and gain information. These features include:

- photos
- subheadings
- maps
- diagrams
- labels
- glossary

Be a Fluent Reader Part of being a fluent reader is reading words correctly. Try this.

- Pick a paragraph that is not too easy or hard.
- Work with a partner. Take turns reading your paragraphs to each other.
- Did you read each word correctly? Use the context of the paragraph to confirm or correct your reading.
- Read your paragraphs until you both read all the words correctly, or with accuracy.

Informational Text Anchor Chart

Features and Graphics

A photo or illustration doesn't usually have labels.

Maps show places mentioned in text.

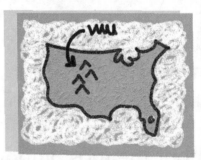

Diagrams label something described in the text.

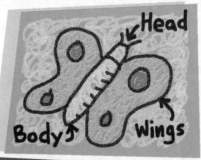

Amazing Migrations: Butterflies, Bats, and Birds

Preview Vocabulary

Look for these words as you read *Amazing Migrations: Butterflies, Bats, and Birds.*

migration	insects	climate	generation	mammal

First Read

Read captions and headings to understand the text.

Look at photos and maps to learn more.

Ask questions to clarify information.

Talk about the most important ideas.

Meet the Author

Cheryl Willis Hudson loves to research and write about science and African American history. When she's not writing books, Cheryl Willis Hudson enjoys creating original quilts.

Amazing Migrations:
Butterflies, Bats, and Birds

by Cheryl Willis Hudson

AUDIO

Audio with Highlighting

ANNOTATE

migration the movement of animals from one habitat to another

1 Some animals live in the same place all year long. Others move to new homes when the seasons change. These animals travel from one habitat to another. This movement is called migration.

salmon

sandhill crane

caribou

Three Animals That Migrate

2   Monarch butterflies, Mexican free-tailed bats, and Arctic terns all migrate. They don't look like each other, but they all fly. They live in different habitats. They travel over long distances. All three animals migrate when the seasons change.

Determine Key Ideas

Use the photos and the heading to decide what the key idea of this section is. Highlight the sentence that tells the key idea.

Monarch butterfly

Mexican free-tailed bat

Arctic tern

<u>Underline</u> the heading that tells you what this section will be about.

insects animals with six legs and three main parts to their bodies

climate the type of weather in a place

Migrating Insects: Monarch Butterflies

3 Monarch butterflies have orange, black, and white wings. During the summer, these insects live in the north. In the fall, the weather becomes cold. They fly south to a warmer climate. In the spring, the butterflies return north.

4   The butterflies that fly south are not the same ones that return in spring. The reason is the butterfly's life span. A life span is how long an animal lives. Most monarchs live only a few weeks. They have a short life span.

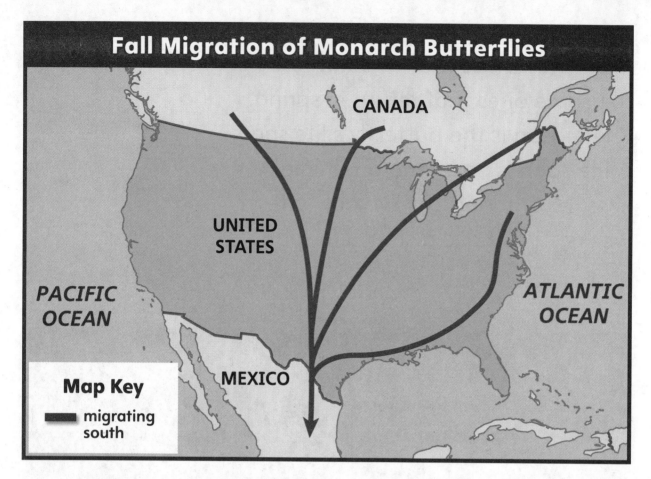

Fall Migration of Monarch Butterflies

CANADA

UNITED STATES

PACIFIC OCEAN

ATLANTIC OCEAN

MEXICO

Map Key

migrating south

CLOSE READ

generation a group of the same animal that is born at the same time

The Super Generation's Journey

5   Each year one generation of monarchs lives longer than the others. A generation is all of the butterflies born at one time. This generation of butterflies lives eight or nine months. In the fall, this super generation migrates. It makes the full journey south.

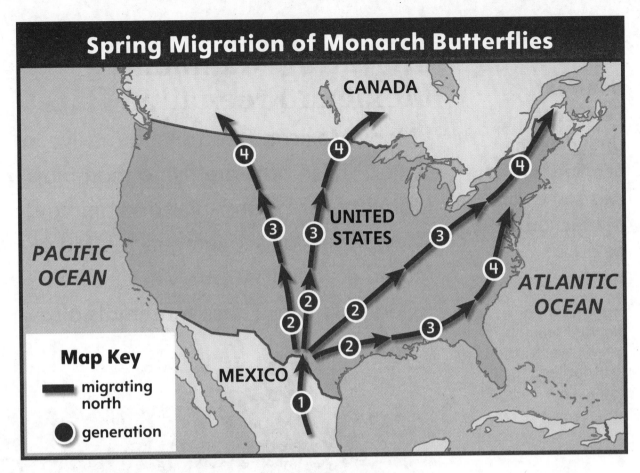

Spring Migration of Monarch Butterflies

CANADA

UNITED STATES

PACIFIC OCEAN

ATLANTIC OCEAN

MEXICO

Map Key

— migrating north

● generation

Many Generations Fly North

6   In the spring, the super generation starts the journey north. It does not get far. The butterflies stop in the southern United States. They lay eggs and die. A new generation is born. These butterflies continue the journey. They go a little farther, lay eggs, and die. This next generation continues the journey. It takes three or four generations to reach their northern home.

CLOSE READ

Determine Key Ideas

Look at the map and the heading. Use what you learn to highlight a key idea on this page.

Use Text Features

<u>Underline</u> the heading that tells you what this section will be about.

mammals warm-blooded animals, often covered with fur, that feed their young with their milk.

Migrating Mammals: Mexican Free-tailed Bats

7   Many Mexican free-tailed bats live in Texas. These bats are flying mammals. Mammals are warm-blooded animals. They are usually covered in fur. Most mammals can't fly, but Mexican free-tailed bats can. These mammals also migrate.

8 Mexican free-tailed bats live in huge colonies. Many colonies are in caves. Sometimes millions of bats live in one cave. At night, they fly out of their homes. They search for food. They eat moths and other insects.

CLOSE READ

Vocabulary in Context

Sometimes pictures can help you understand a word better. Underline the word for a group of free-tailed bats. Look at the photos to help you learn more about the word.

9   Like monarch butterflies, many free-tailed bats fly south for the winter. Their journey starts in the fall. It isn't quite as long as the monarchs' trip. Free-tailed bats travel hundreds of miles. They arrive in Mexico. They stay there for the winter. In the spring, they fly north again.

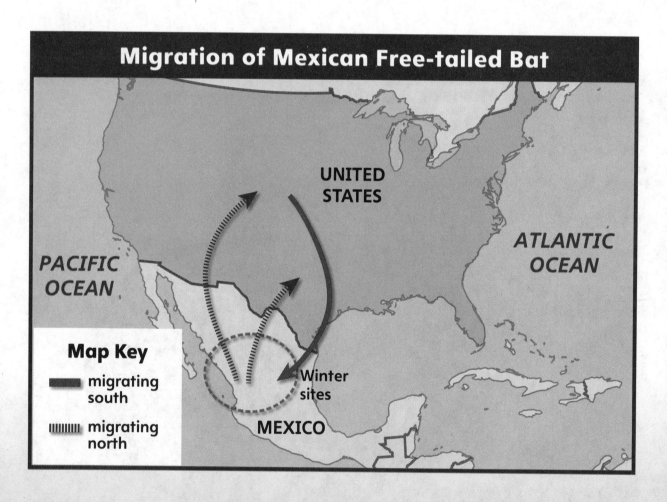

Migration of Mexican Free-tailed Bat

UNITED
STATES

ATLANTIC
OCEAN

PACIFIC
OCEAN

Map Key

▬▬ migrating
south

▥▥ migrating
north

Winter
sites

MEXICO

Migrating Birds: Arctic Terns

10   Arctic terns migrate the longest distance of all animals. They fly more than 35,000 miles round-trip! These terns actually stay in the air for most of their lives. During the summer, they live far up north. Some live near the North Pole or Greenland.

Determine Key Ideas

Highlight details in the text that help you understand the map. Use those details to figure out a key idea on this page.

11 Then Arctic terns migrate to the other end of the world. They fly as far south as Antarctica. This journey is unlike the journey of the bats and the monarchs. Most of the terns' journey is over water. The terns fly thousands of miles over the ocean.

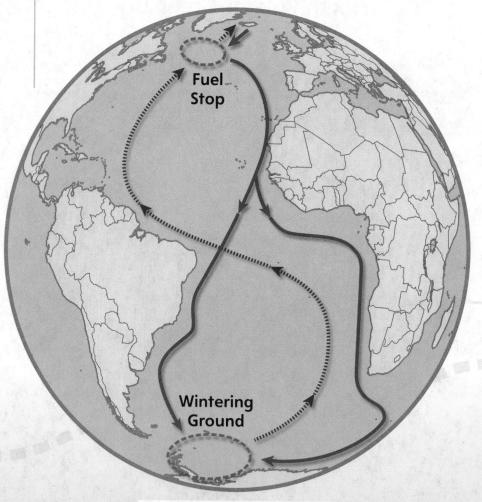

Fuel Stop

Wintering Ground

Map Key

▬▬ migrating south

⦚⦚⦚ migrating north

12　The birds arrive on the ice packs of Antarctica. When the season changes again, the terns head back north. This time, they follow a different route.

Determine Key Ideas

Read the heading and the details in the last paragraph. Use what you learn to highlight a key idea.

Moving with the Seasons

13 Bats, terns, and monarchs know when it's time to migrate. They sense changes in temperature and daylight. They use the position of the sun and stars to find their way. These special skills keep all three animals moving with the seasons.

Glossary

1 **climate** the type of weather in one place

2 **generation** a group of the same animal that is born at the same time

3 **insect** an animal with six legs and three main parts to its body

4 **life span** the time from an animal's birth until its death

5 **mammal** a warm-blooded animal, often covered with fur, that feeds its young with its milk

6 **migration** the movement of animals from one habitat to another

 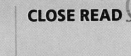

Fluency
Practice reading every word correctly by rereading paragraphs 7–9 aloud several times with a partner.

Develop Vocabulary

MY TURN Use the glossary in *Amazing Migrations* to find each word. Write what each word means. Then discuss the words with a partner. Which words have you heard before? Where? Are any of the words new to you?

Word	Meaning
climate	the type of weather in one place
generation	
insect	
mammal	
migration	

Check for Understanding

MY TURN Write the answers to the questions. Look back at the text to answer the questions.

1. How do you know this is informational text?

_____

_____

_____

_____

2. Why does the author include headings?

_____

_____

_____

_____

_____

_____

3. What pattern do all three animals in the article follow?

_____

_____

_____

_____

Use Text Features

Text features and graphics help readers locate and gain information that supports the author's purpose.

- **Headings** tell what a section is about.

- **Maps** and **diagrams** help clarify the text. They may have **labels** that give important information.

MY TURN Go to the Close Read notes. Underline text features. Use what you underlined to complete the chart.

Text Feature I Underlined	Information It Helped Me Find
Heading: Migrating Insects: Monarch Butterflies	The section is about butterflies.

Determine Key Ideas

Key ideas are the important ideas in a text. As you read, look for text features such as headings, pictures, maps, and diagrams to evaluate details and determine, or find, key ideas.

MY TURN Go back to the Close Read notes. Highlight details that help you find key ideas. Use what you highlight to complete the chart.

Section Title	Key Idea
"Three Animals That Migrate"	Monarch butterflies, Mexican free-tailed bats, and Arctic terns all migrate.
"Many Generations Fly North"	
"Migrating Birds: Arctic Terns"	
"Moving with the Seasons"	

Reflect and Share

Talk About It

This week you read about different animals that migrate. Which animal do you think has the most difficult or challenging journey? Why? Use evidence from the text to support your position.

Disagree Respectfully

During a discussion, you may disagree with classmates' ideas and opinions. It is important to disagree respectfully.

- Keep your voice even.
- Try to find something you agree on.

Use these sentence starters to disagree respectfully.

I agree with you about . . ., but . . .
I see what you mean about . . ., but I also think . . .

Weekly Question

What migration patterns do we see in some animals?

I can use language to make connections between reading and writing informational texts.

Academic Vocabulary

You have learned many new words in this unit.

MY TURN Page through this book or look at the Word Wall. Choose five of your favorite new words, and write them here.

_____   _____

_____   _____

_____   _____

_____

TURN and TALK Share your favorite words from the unit with a partner. Explain why you chose each one. Then use your newly acquired vocabulary to respond to the Essential Question: **What patterns do we see in nature?**

Read Like a Writer, Write for a Reader

Authors use words and graphics such as charts, pictures, and maps for certain purposes. They may want to inform the reader or make an idea clearer. In *Amazing Migrations*, the author used several graphic features.

Graphic Features	Why the Author Included It (Author's Purpose)
maps in the sections "the Super Generation's Journey" and "Many Generations Fly North"	to show where and how far the butterflies go when they migrate
the small round inset photo in the section "Migrating Mammals: Mexican Free-tailed Bats"	to make clear how many bats are crowded into a colony

MY TURN Suppose you are writing about your favorite wild animal. What graphic features would you include with your report?

_____

_____

_____

_____

Spell Words with Long o: o, oa, ow

Long **o** can be spelled **o**, **oa**, or **ow**.

MY TURN Write the Spelling Words that have the same long **o** spelling as each word below. Then write the My Words to Know.

goal

_____

_____

_____

_____

_____

_____

_____

grown

_____

_____

_____

_____

_____

_____

_____

no

_____

_____

_____

My Words to Know

_____

_____

_____

_____

Spelling Words

only

open

float

coach

below

throat

load

throw

bowl

mow

My Words to Know

near

food

Collective Nouns

A **collective noun** names a group of persons or things. It is singular even though it names more than one.

The <u>family</u> <u>is</u> in the park. The <u>family</u> <u>likes</u> the park.

Examples of Collective Nouns				
family	club	team	herd	flock
group	stack	class	band	crowd

MY TURN Edit this draft. Cross out each word you need to change to use a collective noun correctly. Write the correct word above it. The first one is done for you.

> runs
> The team ~~run~~ onto the field. The crowd cheer wildly. My
>
> family sit with me in the stands. We yell too. When the
>
> band play the school song, everyone stands and sings.

I can use elements of informational text to write a list article.

Edit for Commas in a Series

A comma, along with **and** or **or**, separates three or more items in a series, or list.

I love pink, gold, and yellow! Do you prefer blue, green, or red?

Authors edit their writing. They check that they have used commas in lists.

MY TURN Edit this draft. Look for mistakes with commas. Then edit your list article for commas in lists.

A habitat is where a plant, animal͵ or other creature lives.

It provides an animal with food water, and a home. A

habitat can change if the weather turns very hot, cold or

dry. Then some animals migrate.

Edit for Complete Sentences with Subject-Verb Agreement

Complete sentences need a subject and a verb. Subjects and verbs must also agree. Singular subjects often have verbs that end in **-s**. Plural subjects usually do not.

Authors edit their writing to check for complete sentences. They also make sure that subjects and verbs agree.

MY TURN Edit this draft. Check that subjects and verbs agree in complete sentences. Then edit your list article for subject-verb agreement.

> **you**
> Did ^ever see a monarch butterfly? Its colors makes it easy
>
> to spot. A monarch butterfly orange, black, and white
>
> markings. These markings looks pretty, but they also
>
> helps keep the monarch safe. The colors tells enemies
>
> that the monarch has poison in it. If an animal eat a
>
> monarch, the animal get sick. It will be so sick that it
>
> stays away from monarchs after that!

Assessment

In this unit, you learned to write a list article. Rate how well you understand each skill. Review any skill you mark "No."

1. The parts of a list article	YES	NO
2. How to brainstorm ideas	YES	NO
3. How to plan your list article	YES	NO
4. How to develop a topic and main, or central, ideas	YES	NO
5. How to develop details	YES	NO
6. How to write an introduction and a conclusion	YES	NO
7. How to organize details	YES	NO
8. How to use text features such as a title and bold type	YES	NO
9. How to proofread and edit for: • complete sentences with subject-verb agreement • correct use of nouns • commas in series	YES	NO

UNIT THEME

Nature's Wonders

TURN and TALK

Take a Picture With a partner, choose an image in each text that shows a pattern in nature. Write why you chose it. Then use the information to help you answer the Essential Question.

The Seasons of Arnold's Apple Tree

BOOK CLUB

WEEK 2

A Home on the Prairie

BOOK CLUB

WEEK 1

A Green Kid's Guide to Watering Plants

BOOK CLUB

What's in the Egg, Little Pip?

What's in the Egg, Little Pip?

BOOK CLUB

Amazing Migrations: Butterflies, Bats, and Birds

Amazing Migrations: Butterflies, Bats, and Birds

Essential Question

MY TURN

In your notebook, answer the Essential Question: What patterns do we see in nature?

BOOK CLUB

 WEEK 6

Project

Now it is time to apply what you learned about nature's wonders in your **WEEK 6 PROJECT: Tree Bark.**

Compound Words

A **compound word** is made up of two smaller words that form a new word. Use what you know about the smaller words to predict the meaning of a compound word.

bath + tub = bathtub

foot + ball = football

MY TURN Read, or decode, each compound word below. Find the two smaller words in it. Draw a line between the two words.

bedtime	afternoon	everyone	birdbath
classroom	homework	airport	inside
hilltop	moonlight	barnyard	raindrop

TURN and TALK Read these sentences with a partner. Find the compound words. Predict the meaning of each compound word by using the meanings of the smaller words.

I left my notebook on a bookshelf.

I put a bookmark in my book when I stopped reading.

Compound Words

Compound words are words made up of two smaller words.

MY TURN Combine words in the first column with words in the second column to make four compound words. Write each compound word. Then read the words.

sea	box
mail	coat
bird	shell
rain	house

_____

_____

_____

_____

MY TURN Write a sentence with one of the compound words you wrote above.

_____

_____

_____

My Words to Know

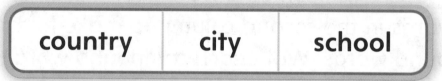 **MY TURN** Read the words in the box. Write the words to complete the sentences.

country	city	school

1. There are many tall buildings in a _city_.

2. You might find farms in the _____.

3. There can be a lot of cars in a _____.

4. Children go to _____ everywhere.

TURN and TALK Work with a partner. Answer the questions.

1. What might you see in the country?

2. What might you see in a city?

3. What do you like best about school?

Spell Compound Words

To spell compound words, think of how the smaller words in each word are spelled.

MY TURN Alphabetize the compound words by writing them in ABC order. Then write My Words to Know.

Spelling Words

weekend	backyard	snowman	driveway	mailbox
raindrop	bathtub	inside	railroad	firefly

1. backyard

2. _____

3. _____

4. _____

5. _____

6. _____

7. _____

8. _____

9. _____

10. _____

My Words to Know

country   school

_____

_____

Tree BARK

Activity

A kindergarten teacher wants you to share facts about tree bark with her class. Make tree rubbings and write a fact sheet to share with the kindergarten class. Point out facts about the patterns in the bark.

Let's Read!

This week you will read three texts about patterns in nature. Today's article will help you build background knowledge.

1. Looking at Tree Bark
2. Tidal Patterns
3. Nature's Skyscrapers

Generate Questions

COLLABORATE With a partner, talk about how to make a tree rubbing. Think of two questions to guide your research on tree bark.

Use Academic Words

COLLABORATE Talk about the picture with your partner. Respond using your new academic vocabulary words. Be sure to use these words in your fact sheet.

Academic Vocabulary

behavior	identify
design	similar
evidence	

Tree Bark Research Plan

Follow this research plan with help from your teacher.

Day 1 List questions for research.

Day 2 Make tree rubbings and do research on tree bark. Take notes as you read about trees.

Day 3 Write a fact sheet for the kindergarten class.

Day 4 Revise and edit your fact sheet.

Day 5 Present your tree rubbings and fact sheet to your classmates.

Know the Facts

An informational text has

- one main, or central, idea
- key details that tell about the main idea
- facts and examples

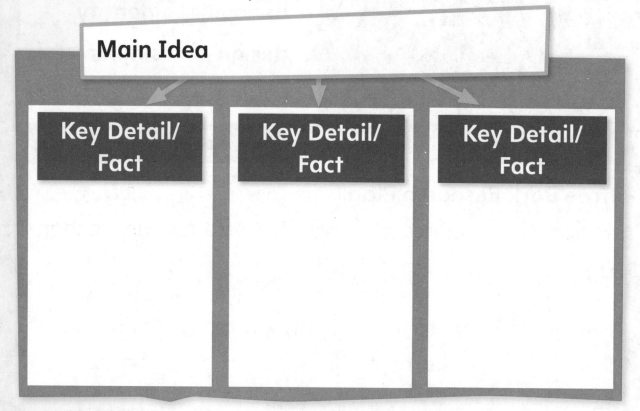

COLLABORATE With a partner, read "Tidal Patterns." Work with your class to fill in the chart.

Main Idea

Key Detail/ Fact	Key Detail/ Fact	Key Detail/ Fact

After you read an informational text, think about the facts you read. How could you make sure they are true?

_____

- -

_____

Identify and Gather Relevant Sources

Books in the library can be good sources. Use the **database** to find books to use as sources. Type in the topic of your fact sheet as the keyword.

 PUBLIC LIBRARY

| Trees | |

You will get many books to choose from. How do you pick the best one? Read the title and summary for each book. Then find some books and look through them. Look at headings, photos, and words in bold print.

To demonstrate that you understand the information gathered, ask yourself, "Is this source helpful? Will this book tell facts about my main idea? Did it answer my questions and do I understand the answers?"

COLLABORATE Look at these books from a library database. Underline the books that might have facts about tree bark. Explain why you chose them and why they are relevant.

- Planting Trees in Your Garden
- Family Tree
- Trees
- Trees: Poetry

Fact Sheet

In a fact sheet, the writer gives important information about a topic by listing the main, or central, idea and key facts from sources. The writer may include a picture too.

Central Idea

Spirals in Nature

Facts from Source(s)

Sunflowers

- Seeds grow in a spiral.
- The spiral holds the seeds together.

Leaves

- Leaves grow in a spiral.
- The spiral allows all leaves to get sunlight.

Visual

Paraphrasing

You need to put the facts from sources in your own words. That's called paraphrasing. Follow these steps to paraphrase:

1. Read a fact in a book. Then close the book.

2. In your own words, tell what you read.

3. When you use your own words, be sure you keep the same meaning as the words in the book.

COLLABORATE Read the fact below. Then paraphrase it.

Fact from source: Bark is the outer covering on a tree. Although bark from different trees can look different, bark protects the tree.

Source: Garden Guide

My paraphrase:

_____

_____

_____

_____

Create a Poster with Images

Fact sheets often have images, such as photos, like the fact sheet **Spirals in Nature.** You can also include a diagram or chart to make your fact sheet stronger.

A diagram can help readers see parts of a whole item. This diagram shows how to count the spirals in a sunflower.

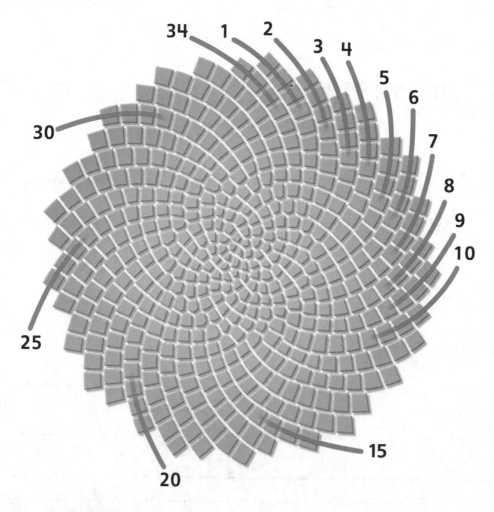

COLLABORATE With a partner, make a poster of your fact sheet. Choose images to include.

Revise

COLLABORATE Read your fact sheet to your partner. Discuss what is good and what might be improved. Then listen to your partner's fact sheet and offer feedback.

Did you check your		
central idea?	yes	no
facts from sources?	yes	no
images?	yes	no

Edit

COLLABORATE Read your fact sheet again.

Check for

☐ spelling

☐ punctuation

☐ subject-verb agreement

Share

COLLABORATE Share your fact sheet with others. Present your poster. Ask for questions and comments. Remember to follow these rules for speaking and listening:

- Respond to questions with more than one word.

- Listen actively, asking questions to make sure you understand the speaker.

Now post your fact sheet so that others may read it.

Reflect

MY TURN Complete the sentences.

As I worked on my fact sheet, I most enjoyed

_____

- -

_____

One thing I think is good about my fact sheet is

_____

- -

_____

- -

_____

Reflect on Your Goals

Look back at your unit goals. Use a different color to rate yourself again.

 Complete the sentences.

Reflect on Your Reading

From independent reading in this unit, I most liked

_____

- -

_____

- -

_____

Reflect on Your Writing

My best writing from this unit is

_____

- -

_____

- -

_____

How to Use a Glossary

This **glossary** tells you what a word in this book means and how to say it. The words are in ABC order. **Guide words** at the top of each page show the first and last words on the page. To find a word, think about how it is spelled. Look up the first letter of the word to find it. If a word you are looking for is not in this glossary, use a print or online **dictionary**. To use an online dictionary, type the word in the search box.

The pronunciation guide shows you how to say the word.

Ff

flock (FLOK) A **flock** is a group of animals of the same kind. NOUN

All words that begin with **f** will be after **Ff**.

This sentence tells you what the word means.

TURN and **TALK** Find the word **climate** in the glossary. On a piece of paper, write its meaning. Write a sentence using the word. Decide how to say it. Then work together to find a word in an online dictionary. Find its meaning and how to say it.

Aa

affect (uh FEKT) To **affect** something is to have an effect on it or to change it in some way. VERB

arrange (uh RAYNJ) When you **arrange** something, you put it in some kind of order. VERB

Bb

backyard (BAK YARD) A **backyard** is a yard behind a house or building. NOUN

behavior (bi HAY vyer) The **behavior** of a person or animal is how that person or animal acts. NOUN

burrows (BER ohz) **Burrows** are holes or tunnels in the ground that are made by a small animal. NOUN

Cc

carefully (KAIR fuhl ee) If you do something **carefully**, you do it with thought and close attention. ADVERB certain • decorates

certain (SERT uhn) **Certain** can mean some, but not all. ADJECTIVE

climate (KLY mit) **Climate** is the type of weather in one place. NOUN

colonies (KOL uh neez) **Colonies** are groups of animals that live in one place. NOUN

community (kuh MYOO nuh tee) A **community** is a place where people live, work, and play. Stores, houses, and libraries are all part of a community. NOUN

compare (kuhm PAIR) When you **compare** people or things, you find out or point out how people or things are alike and how they are different. VERB

Dd

daylight (DAY lyt) **Daylight** is the natural light of day. NOUN

decorates (DEK uh rayts) If someone **decorates**, he or she makes something look pretty by putting something on it. VERB

design (di ZYN) A **design** is an arrangement of details, form, and color in a painting, building, or part of nature. NOUN

different (DIF er uhnt) When two things are **different**, they are not alike. ADJECTIVE

Ee

evidence (EV uh duhns) **Evidence** is anything that proves what happened. NOUN

excited (ek SY tid) When you are **excited**, you have very strong, happy feelings about something that you like. ADJECTIVE

explore (ek SPLOR) When you **explore**, you look around a place to learn things. VERB

Ff

favorite (FAY ver it) Your **favorite** thing is the one you like better than all the others. ADJECTIVE

flock (FLOK) A **flock** is a group of animals of the same kind. NOUN

Gg

generation (jen uh RAY shuhn) A **generation** is a group of people or animals that is born at the same time. NOUN

glow (GLOH) To **glow** is to shine or put out light. VERB

grazers (GRAY zerz) **Grazers** are animals that feed on growing grasses. NOUN

guide (GYD) A **guide** is a person who shows people around. NOUN

Hh

habitat (HAB uh tat) A **habitat** is a place where a plant or an animal usually lives. NOUN

hospital (HOSS pi tuhl) A **hospital** is a place where doctors and nurses care for sick or injured people. NOUN

huddled (HUD uhld) If you **huddled**, you moved very close to something or someone else. VERB

Ii

identify (eye DEN tuh fy) To **identify** is to recognize, tell, or prove who or what something is. VERB

insects (IN sektz) **Insects** are small animals with six legs and three main parts to their bodies. NOUN

Jj

joy (JOI) **Joy** is a feeling of great happiness. NOUN

Ll

librarian (ly BRAIR ee uhn) A **librarian** is a person who is in charge of or helps to run a library. NOUN

location (loh KAY shuhn) A **location** is a position or place. NOUN

lonely (LOHN lee) If you are **lonely,** you feel sad because you are alone. ADJECTIVE

Mm

mammals (MAM uhlz) **Mammals** are warm-blooded animals, often covered with fur, that feed their young with their milk. NOUN

might (MYT) **Might** is power or strength. NOUN

migration (my GRAY shuhn) **Migration** is the movement of animals from one habitat to another. NOUN

moist (MOIST) Something that is **moist** is slightly wet. ADJECTIVE

Oo

oval (OH vuhl) Something that is **oval** has the shape of an egg. ADJECTIVE

Pp

penguin (PEN gwin) A **penguin** is a short-legged, black-and-white seabird that cannot fly and that lives in or near the Antarctic. NOUN

place (PLAYSS) To **place** something is to put or set it down. VERB

prairie (PRAIR ee) A **prairie** is a large, open grassland with very few trees. NOUN

Qq

quietly (KWY uht lee) To do something **quietly** is to do it so that it does not make noise. ADVERB

Rr

region (REE juhn) A **region** is any place, space, or area. NOUN

rhythm (RITH uhm) **Rhythm** is the strong beat that some music or poetry has. NOUN

rustle (RUS uhl) To **rustle** is to make a soft sound of things rubbing together. VERB

Ss

scolding (SKOHLD ing) **Scolding** is speaking in an angry way. VERB

scurried (SKER eed) **Scurried** means moved quickly. VERB

searchlights (SERCH lyts) **Searchlights** are powerful lights that can shine in any direction. NOUN

services (SER vis iz) **Services** are things that people do to help others. NOUN

shadows (SHAD ohz) **Shadows** are shaded places away from light. NOUN

similar (SIM uh ler) Two things are **similar** if they are alike or almost alike in some way. ADJECTIVE

soggy (SOG ee) If something is **soggy**, it is very wet. ADJECTIVE

splattered (SPLAT erd) To be **splattered** means to be splashed by dots of something. ADJECTIVE

spread (SPRED) To **spread** is to stretch out or apart. VERB

stamp (STAMP) When you **stamp**, you put a foot down forcefully. VERB

supermarkets (SOO per mar kits) **Supermarkets** are large stores that sell food and other goods. NOUN

Tt

tour (TUR) A **tour** is a visit to see things. NOUN

treehouse (TREE howss) A **treehouse** is a small space built in the branches of a tree for children to play in or on. NOUN

Ww

waddle (WAD uhl) To **waddle** is to walk with short steps while swinging the body from side to side. VERB

ABDO Publishing Company
A Green Kid's Guide to Watering Plants by Richard M Lay, Copyright ABDO Publishing.

Brooks Permissions
"Pete at the Zoo," reprinted By Consent of Brooks Permissions.

HarperCollins Publishers
"Keziah," Copyright ©1956 by Gwendolyn Brooks Blakely. Used by permission of HarperCollins Publishers. This selection may not be re-illustrated without written permission of HarperCollins. "Rudolph Is Tired of the City," Copyright ©1956 by Gwendolyn Brooks Blakely. Used by permission of HarperCollins Publishers. This selection may not be re-illustrated without written permission of HarperCollins. "Lyle," Copyright ©1956 by Gwendolyn Brooks Blakely. Used by permission of HarperCollins Publishers. This selection may not be re-illustrated without written permission of HarperCollins.

Houghton Mifflin Harcourt Publishing Company
Maybe Something Beautiful: How Art Transformed a Neighborhood by F. Isabel Campoy and Theresa Howell, illustrated by Rafael Lopez. Text copyright© 2016 by F. Isabel Campoy and Theresa Howell. Illustrations copyright© 2016 by Rafael Lopez. Reprinted by permission of Houghton Mifflin Harcourt Publishing Company. All rights reserved. *The Seasons of Arnold's Apples* by Gail Gibbons. Copyright© 2016 by Gail Gibbons. Reprinted by permission of Houghton Mifflin Harcourt Publishing Company. All rights reserved.

Red Chair Press
Places We Go: A Kids' Guide to Community Buildings by Rachel Kreisman © Red Chair Press LLC. Used with permission.

Scholastic Library Publishing
A Home on the Prairie by David C. Lion. All rights reserved. Reprinted by permission of Children's Press an imprint of Scholastic Library Publishing, Inc.

Simon & Schuster, Inc.
WHAT'S IN THE EGG, LITTLE PIP by Karma Wilson, illustrated by Jane Chapman, Text copyright © 2010 by Karma Wilson. Illustrations copyright © 2010 by Jane Chapman. Reprinted with permission of Margaret K. McElderry Books, an Imprint of Simon & Schuster Children's Publishing Division. All rights reserved.

Writers House LLC.
WHAT'S IN THE EGG, LITTLE PIP by Karma Wilson, illustrated by Jane Chapman, Margaret K. McElderry Books an Imprint of Simon & Schuster Children's Publishing Division, 1230 Avenue of the Americas, New York, New York 10020. Text copyright © 2010 by Karma Wilson. Illustrations copyright © 2010 by Jane Chapman. All rights reserved.

Photographs
Photo locators denoted as follows Top (T), Center (C), Bottom (B), Left (L), Right (R), Background (Bkgd)

4 KAD Photo/Shutterstock; **6** Larry Geddis/Alamy Stock Photo; **8** (BL) Monkey Business Images/Shutterstock, (Bkgd) Gagliardi Images/Shutterstock; **9** KAD Photo/Shutterstock; **13** (BL) James R. Martin/Shutterstock, (BR) Anurak Pongpatimet/Shutterstock; **14** Fotokvadrat/Shutterstock; **15** (BR) ESB Professional/Shutterstock, (TR) Sergey Novikov/Shutterstock; **16** (BC) Pogonici/Shutterstock, (BL) Holbox/Shutterstock, (BR) Lucian Milasan/123RF, (TL) Jill Lang/Shutterstock, (TR) DenisNata/Shutterstock; **17** Angelo Gilardelli/Shutterstock; **18** (BC) SeDmi/Shutterstock, (BL) Pincarel/Shutterstock, (BR) Vereshchagin Dmitry/Shutterstock, (C) Kkulikov/Shutterstock, (CL) Eric Isselee/Shutterstock, (CR) Morenina/Shutterstock, (TC) Tsekhmister/Shutterstock, (TL) DenisNata/Shutterstock, (TR) Serezniy/123RF; **54** (BC) R. Classen/Shutterstock, (BR) Wire_man/Shutterstock, (BL) Eric Isselee/Shutterstock, (TL) Rsooll/Shutterstock, (TR) Happydancing/Shutterstock; **55** Tatik22/Shutterstock; **60** Used with permission from the author; **89** Monkey Business Images/Shutterstock; **90** (C) Flashon Studio/123RF, (Bkgd) Lightkite/Shutterstock; **91** Prath/Shutterstock; **92** (BL) Stefan Glebowski/Shutterstock, (BR) Karina Bakalyan/Shutterstock, (C) Morenina/Shutterstock, (CL) Oksana Perkins/Shutterstock, (CR) Civdis/Shutterstock, (TL) STILLFX/Shutterstock, (TR) 123RF; **94** (BC) Christopher Ray Robertson/Shutterstock, (BL) Stockphoto Mania/Shutterstock, (BR) Eric Isselee/Shutterstock, (TC) 123RF, (TL) Africa Studio/Shutterstock, (TR) Szefei/123RF; **98** Used with permission from Red Chair Press; **99** KAD Photo/Shutterstock; **101** Albert Pego/Shutterstock; **102** Monkey Business Images/Shutterstock; **103** Pressmaster/Shutterstock; **104** Antonio Diaz/123RF**105** Monkey Business Images/Shutterstock; **106** Jamie Pham/Alamy Stock Photo; **107** (C) Rob Marmion/Shutterstock, (T) Tyler Olson/123RF; **108** Robert Kneschke/Alamy Stock Photo; **109** Wavebreak Media Ltd/123RF; **110** Blend Images/Shutterstock; **111** Cathy Yeulet/123RF; **112** ESB Professional/Shutterstock; **113** Mr Doomits/Alamy Stock Photo; **114** Cathy Yeulet/123RF**115** Paulaphoto/Shutterstock; **128** Oneinchpunch/Shutterstock; **129** Lakhesis/123RF; **130** (BC) Agorohov/Shutterstock, (BL) Kruglov Orda/Shutterstock, (BR) V.S. Anandhakrishna/Shutterstock, (TL) Paleka/Shutterstock, (TR) Coprid/Shutterstock; **131** (C) Africa Studio/Shutterstock, (CL) Shuai Jie Guo/Shutterstock, (CR) Polryaz/Shutterstock, (TC) Oleksiy Mark/Shutterstock, (TL) Steshkin Yevgeniy/Shutterstock, (TR) Richard Peterson/Shutterstock; **136** Everett Collection Inc/Alamy Stock Photo; **137** © 2019 Faith Ringgold / Artists Rights Society (ARS), New York, Courtesy ACA Galleries, New York; **158** (Bkgd) Pung/Shutterstock, (TR) Zhukova Valentyna/

Shutterstock; **159** (Bkgd) Jason Maehl/Shutterstock, (C) Anton Foltin/Shutterstock; **160** (BL) MaraZe/Shutterstock, (BC) R. Classen/Shutterstock, (BR) Pratchaya.Lee/Shutterstock, (CL) StockPhotosArt/Shutterstock, (TL) Le Do/Shutterstock, (TR) Voronin76/Shutterstock; **161** Ann Baldwin/Shutterstock; **196** (CL) Khoroshunova Olga/Shutterstock, (CR) Dja65/Shutterstock, (TL) Adisa/Shutterstock, (TR) Kitch Bain/123RF; **197** (BC) Server/123RF, (BL) Irina Fischer/Shutterstock, (BR) Rowena/Shutterstock, (TC) Fiphoto/123RF, (TL) Danny Smythe/Shutterstock, (TR) Whitepointer/123RF; **200** Senatorek/Shutterstock; **206** (BL) Monkey Business Images/Shutterstock, (CL) Felix Lipov/Shutterstock; **210** (Bkgd) Milosz_G/Shutterstock, (BL) Natdive/Shutterstock; **211** Larry Geddis/Alamy Stock Photo; **215** (BC) Sumikophoto/Shutterstock, (BL) Wuttichok Painichiwarapun/Shutterstock, (BR) AdStock RF/Shutterstock; **218** (BC) Karkas/Shutterstock, (BL) Gyvafoto/Shutterstock, (BR) Chones/Shutterstock, (CL) Iakov Kalinin/Shutterstock, (CR) Daniel Prudek/Shutterstock, (TL) Morenina/Shutterstock, (TR) MIA Studio/Shutterstock; **253** Steve Byland/Shutterstock; **256** (Bkgd) Weldon Schloneger/Shutterstock, (BL) Ksenia Ragozina/Shutterstock, (BR) Cathy Withers-Clarke/Shutterstock, (CL) Geoffrey Kuchera/Shutterstock, (CR) Aureliy/Shutterstock; **257** (BL) Christopher Elwell/Shutterstock, (TL) Weldon Schloneger/Shutterstock; **258** (BL) Ajt/Shutterstock, (BR) Testing/Shutterstock, (CL) Africa Studio/Shutterstock, (CR) Givaga/Shutterstock, (TL) Vitolef/123RF, (TR) Jill Lang/Shutterstock; **265** (Bkgd) Larry Geddis/Alamy Stock Photo, (BL) Rolf Nussbaumer/Nature Picture Library/Alamy Stock Photo, (BR) Avalon/Photoshot License/Alamy Stock Photo, (BC) Art Wolfe/Science Source; **266** Rolf Nussbaumer/Nature Picture Library/Alamy Stock Photo; **267** Larry Geddis/Alamy Stock Photo **268** Steve Cooper/Science Source; **269** Art Wolfe/Science Source; **270** Kerry Hargrove/Shutterstock; **271** Craig K. Lorenz/Science Source; **272** AvalonPhotoshot License/Alamy Stock Photo; **273** Laura Romin & Larry Dalton/Alamy Stock Photo; **274** (BR) Gary Meszaros/Avalon/Bruce Coleman Inc/Alamy Stock Photo, (T) Nature's Images/Science Source; **275** (B) Bill Draker/Rolf Nussbaumer Photography/Alamy Stock Photo, (T) Jim Zipp/Science Source; **276** Kerry Hargrove/Shutterstock; **277** Steve Cooper/Science Source; **292** (BL) 123RF, (BR) Mary Rice/Shutterstock, (CL) Civdis/Shutterstock, (CR) Stefan Glebowski/Shutterstock, (TC) Kkulikov/Shutterstock, (TL) 123RF, (TR) Africa Studio/Shutterstock; **294** (C) Andrey Kuzmin/Shutterstock, (CL) Monkey Business Images/Shutterstock, (CR) Vita Khorzhevska/Shutterstock, (TC) Billion Photos/Shutterstock, (TL) Nattika/Shutterstock, (TR) Terekhov Igor/Shutterstock; **298** Used with permission from Gail Gibbons; **334** (Bkgd) Alexey Osokin/Shutterstock, (BL) Oksana Golubeva/Shutterstock, (C) Fitzthum Photography/Shutterstock, (TL) tamsindove/Shutterstock; **336** Angelo Gilardelli/

Shutterstock, (BC) Morenina/Shutterstock, (BR) Stefan Glebowski/Shutterstock, (T) DenisNata/Shutterstock; **342** Used with permission from Simon & Schuster, Inc.; **378** (BR) Joe Morris 917/Shutterstock, (CR) DavidHoffmann photography/Shutterstock; **379** Efimova Anna/Shutterstock; **380** (CL) Lucadp/Shutterstock, (C) Lestertair/Shutterstock, (CR) Stephen VanHorn/Shutterstock, (T) KKulikov/Shutterstock; **381** (TC) Vitolef/123RF, (TL) Ashas0612/Shutterstock, (TR) Eric Isselee/Shutterstock; **387** (Bkgd) Noradoa/Shutterstock, (BL) Halldore/Shutterstock, (C) Merlin D. Tuttle/Science Source, (CL) StevenRussellSmithPhotos/Shutterstock; **388** (Bkgd) Design Pics Inc/Alamy Stock Photo, (BL) Design Pics Inc/Alamy Stock Photo, (BR) Joe Ferrer/Shutterstock, (CR) Epicscotland/Alamy Stock Photo; **389** (BL) Halldore/Shutterstock, (CL) Steven Russell SmithPhotos/Shutterstock, (CR) Merlin D. Tuttle/Science Source; **390** James Laurie/Shutterstock; **391** Naturalv/123RF; **394** (Bkgd) Gillian Lloyd/Alamy Stock Photo, (CL) Rick & Nora Bowers/Alamy Stock Photo; **395** Tom Uhlman/Alamy Stock Photo; **397** Bill Coster/Alamy Stock Photo; **399** Blickwinkel/Alamy Stock Photo; **400** (Bkgd) Reisegraf.ch/Alamy Stock Photo, (C) Butterfly Hunter/Shutterstock; **401** (BL) Blickwinkel/Alamy Stock Photo, (BR) Merlin D. Tuttle/Science Source, (CR) James Laurie/Shutterstock; **416** (TR) Denis Pepin/Shutterstock, (TC) stocksolutions/Shutterstock; **420** Vladimir Wrangel/Shutterstock; **424** (BL) AdStock RF/Shutterstock, (BR) Paggi Eleanor/Shutterstock.

Illustrations

21, 50, 59, 97, 135, 165 Ken Bowser; **23–39** James E. Ransome; **52–53** André Jolicoeur; **61–77** Rafael López; **137, 140–145** Faith Ringgold; **138–139** Barbara Schaffer; **167–181** Steve Cox; **206** Rob Schuster; **216–217** André Jolicoeur; **223, 263, 297, 341, 385** Ken Bowser; **225–243** Laura Zarrin; **290–291** André Jolicoeur; **299–321** Gail Gibbons; **343–365** Jane Chapman; **423, 426** Rob Schuster.